PRAISE FOR *SCHOLAR[illegible]*
THE IMPORTANCE OF CHILD PLAY AS A HUMAN RIGHT

"*Scholarly Snapshots* is an indispensable jumping off point for anyone seeking to understand the power and vitality of play, not only as the primary mechanism through which children learn but also as a human right. This concise survey of the work and insights of many of the most important foundational thinkers in the world of play—from Froebel and Dewey to present day scholars—is essential reading for anyone who takes play seriously."—**Tom Hobson, "Teacher Tom," educator, writer, international speaker, and author of *Teacher Tom's First Book* and *Teacher Tom's Second Book***

"Dr. Vivien L. Geneser and colleagues defend and deeply explore the child's right to play in this exciting book. From perspectives of historical and contemporary theorists, play is given the reverence that it deserves. This is the text I, as a professor of early childhood education, will use in my courses to help future teachers of young children, brain architects, gain the knowledge they need in the twenty-first century to advocate for every child's right to play."—**Zlata Stanković-Ramirez, Assistant Professor, Early Childhood Education, Coastal Carolina University**

"This book is essential for my early childhood library as a mother, grandmother, teacher educator, and human being. Beginning with the title: play as a human right, we learn about the history of play from every angle, knowledge of development, pedagogy, and human experience, and I am inspired to fight for children's right to play. Indeed, I am reminded again and again that we stand on the shoulders of our founding fathers and mothers of early childhood development and education. There are way too many quotes in the book for me to share, but I conclude with Gesell's quote from the book: 'When a child is playing, he concentrates with his whole being and acquires emotional satisfactions which he cannot get from other forms of activities."—**Tamar Jacobson, PhD, author of *Everyone Needs Attention: Helping Young Children Thrive***

"This collection is a much-needed counter to the current atmosphere in education of pushing academics earlier and earlier. Children need to play to learn."—**Suzanne Roth Fulton, retired public school teacher, mom, and grandmother**

"So inspiring. A quick, enticing, helpful read. Brilliant format. Wonderful to see a historical overview, which then sparks your own ideas for which ideas you could adopt and use."—**Derek Sivers, author of *How to Live and Anything You Want***

"For those who have committed to taking schools into new territories with more just ways to learn, it is vitally important to know the past. *Scholarly Snapshots* walks us through the past, beginning with early explorations of the actions of the young up to those more recent contributors to thoughts on encounters in school, the common thread being the elusive endeavor we call 'play.' There are notable subtexts in this important collection that are not hard to read, from the exclusion of all but masculine pronouns in scholars' writings on play for the first three hundred years up to the very late appearance of the voices of women of color in scholarship. Along the way are shifting and interconnected notions on what we so casually call play. The common thread? That we must take seriously what children choose: play. This volume explores the serious thought that researchers, theorists, and educators have put to what the young choose to do—whether that choice is joyful or brings conflict, creative or reproductive of injustices, democratic or demagogic, chimeric or characterizable, students choose to play. It is vital that teachers, researchers, administrators, parents, and policymakers understand the centuries-worth of scholarship about what human beings do from the start: we play. What does a complicated understanding of play help us do? Move forward into those territories with more just ways to learn."—**Timothy A. Kinard, PhD, Associate Professor, early education, Texas State University, College of Education, Department of Curriculum and Instruction**

"This collection of the histories of play scholars and their contributions written by contemporary play advocates is a much-needed treasure. Just as the book title promises, each chapter provides a brief yet rich description of the scholar, their work, and its context in portions that are manageable for undergraduate students. As a teacher educator, I am eager to bring this book into my Play course to help preservice teachers appreciate the deep history of play and its diverse voices. The illustrations add a lovely touch to each chapter!"—**Deepti Kharod, PhD, Assistant Professor, Teacher Education, University of the Incarnate Word Chair, Dr. Joe L. Frost Play Research Collection Advisory Board**

Scholarly Snapshots

Scholarly Snapshots

The Importance of Child Play as a Human Right

Edited by
Vivien L. Geneser

ROWMAN & LITTLEFIELD
Lanham • Boulder • New York • London

Published by Rowman & Littlefield
An imprint of The Rowman & Littlefield Publishing Group, Inc.
4501 Forbes Boulevard, Suite 200, Lanham, Maryland 20706
www.rowman.com

86-90 Paul Street, London EC2A 4NE, United Kingdom

British Library Cataloguing in Publication Information Available

Library of Congress Cataloging-in-Publication Data

Names: Geneser, Vivien L., 1954- editor.
Title: Scholarly snapshots : the importance of child play as a human right / edited by Vivien L. Geneser.
Description: Lanham, Maryland : Rowman & Littlefield, [2022] | Includes bibliographical references. | Summary: "Within this book, you will read content from familiar theorists and, hopefully, discover new ways of thinking about play"—Provided by publisher.
Identifiers: LCCN 2021059277 (print) | LCCN 2021059278 (ebook) | ISBN 9781475843187 (Cloth : acid-free paper) | ISBN 9781475843194 (Paperback : acid-free paper) | ISBN 9781475843200 (ePub)
Subjects: LCSH: Play. | Child development. | Children's rights.
Classification: LCC LB1137 .S323 2022 (print) | LCC LB1137 (ebook) | DDC 372.21—dc23/eng/20220209
LC record available at https://lccn.loc.gov/2021059277
LC ebook record available at https://lccn.loc.gov/2021059278

∞™ The paper used in this publication meets the minimum requirements of American National Standard for Information Sciences—Permanence of Paper for Printed Library Materials, ANSI/NISO Z39.48-1992.

In loving memory of
Joe L. Frost
1933–2020

Former President of IPAUSA
International Play Association-United States Affiliate

For Allison, Tom, Ben, David, and the memory of John Geneser.

Contents

Foreword

Josh Thompson

Play is important to children. Many reliable sources confirm this statement: theorists, practitioners, classroom teachers, teacher educators, and writers. But the most reliable source is children themselves. Children play because it is fun! But it also benefits them in every domain of their development. Perhaps most significant is how play amplifies and improves relations between children and their peers, caregivers, and teachers. Play humanizes that relationship, and provides space to both grow and learn.

The book in your hand, or on your screen, gathers 16 theorists from diverse spaces to see what they each have to say about play. From deep in the eighteenth century until contemporary times, across cultures and different disciplines, through many languages, these theorists observed children in their finest form, at play. From social interactions to meaningful engagements, beginning in the crib, and outside to the playing field and forest, these theorists examined the evidence before them. Each in their own way, they affirmed that play is at the center of childhood growth and development.

The authors recruited by Dr. Vivien Geneser, coeditor of *Scholarly Snapshots*, brought pertinent expertise and talent to their storytelling. The connections between each of these authors and their scholars center around a joint fascination with the child at play. The text of these *Scholarly Snapshots* tells the tale of childlike wonder and love of learning.

This text may find its roost on the shelves of scholars, each on their own pursuit of understanding the child at play. But it also comes to life in the classrooms of teacher educators and trainers as they consider the pertinence and applicability of each theorist. The teachers of tomorrow need to know what these theorists have to say about children, their development, and how they grow and learn. But the most important lesson for teachers of these children that will grow up and live into the twenty-second century is that wise students of the child have long celebrated the child's right to play!

Acknowledgments

Many people contributed to the compilation of these vignettes that portray great thinkers and their thoughts on play. First, I would like to extend gratitude to Allison Geneser and Benjamin Geneser, who contributed the beautiful images.

Next, thanks to A&M-SA colleagues, Theresa Garfield, Michael Boucher, Karen Burgard, Carl Sheperis, Armando Tejeda, Zlata Stanković-Ramirez, Scott Peters, Evelyn Villarreal, and Lawrence Scott. Special thanks to Prairie Lea pals, Charles Wright, Shawna Pooley, Lulu Ivarra, and the Teacher Tribe. Thanks to dear friends Manice Massengale, Carolyn Appleton, Barbara Chaffe, Sue Bean, Lisa Thompson, Suzanne Fulton, Deborah Paulus-Jagric, Margie Currie-Wood, Holly Noelke, Ginger Lowry, Susan Montana, Elizabeth Blood, Barbara Kelly, Karen Monteith, Elayne Lansford, Kimberly Scheberle, and Mary Irvine.

Thanks to the chapter authors, Mary Ruth Moore, LaDonna Atkins, Josh Thompson, David J. Akpata, Marcy Guddemi, Blythe Hinitz, Jeroen Staring, Jerry Aldridge, Olga Jarrett, Joanna Cemore Brigden, Deb Lawrence, Karen Walker, Shelley Harris, Walter Drew, Debora Wisneski, John Sutterby, Kenya Wolff, Edith Esparza, Matilde A. Sarmiento, Jerletha McDonald, and Reece Wilson.

Thanks to the editorial team at Rowman & Littlefield: Tom Koerner, Carlie Wall, and Megan DeLancey, who provided consistent encouragement.

Thank you to my mother, Pamela Woods Loomis, who celebrated her ninety-ninth birthday in 2021. Thanks to my siblings and cousins who took care of Mom during her final days.

Thanks also, to you, dear reader, for your interest in the study of play and for exploring our book: *Scholarly Snapshots: The Importance of Child Play as a Human Right*.

One hundred percent of the proceeds from this book will be donated to the International Play Association–United States Affiliate.

www.ipa.usa

Introduction

Vivien L. Geneser

Welcome to *Scholarly Snapshots: The Importance of Child Play as a Human Right*. Whether you are an educator, parent, or student, we hope that you enjoy these snapshots: brief glimpses into the ways that notable thinkers perceive the value of play. The authors of these chapters are professors, educators, child development specialists, and ardent advocates of the child's right to play. We were alarmed by the cultural decline of play, especially in schools, due to the increase in use of technology, reduction of recess, and emphasis on testing. Thus, we mobilized to generate a collection of insights from notable theorists and educators who have emphasized play as an integral aspect of healthy human development.

Within this book, you will read content from familiar theorists and, hopefully, discover new ways of thinking about play. As collaborators, we wanted to bring together a wide range of intellectuals from different eras to highlight the fact that the value of play has been recognized for many years. In the process of selecting scholars to feature, we have undoubtedly omitted some of your favorites, but it would be impossible to include all of the influential proponents of play in this slim volume. However, we aspire to pique your interest in the perspective of these sixteen impressive scholars with the hope that you will continue to pursue your own interest in play and, perhaps, become an advocate.

Thanks again to all of my fellow play enthusiasts!

1

Friedrich Froebel

1782–1852

Mary Ruth Moore

Friedrich Froebel.

The plays of childhood are the germinal leaves of all later life.

Imagine if you would, a child building with wooden blocks, stacking block upon block until she creates a wall. Next, see the image of brick masons laying the first cornerstone for a new building and then, brick by brick, the wall of a great building takes shape. These mental images ready you for thinking about Friedrich Froebel, who literally laid the cornerstone for play as a method of learning, assuring that all children have the right to play from a very early age. Froebel's cornerstone was child-centered play and his whole life attested to this objective.

FATHER OF KINDERGARTEN

Friedrich Froebel, known as the Father of Kindergarten, was born on April 21, 1782, in Oberweissbach, a small town in central Germany. Froebel's mother died before his first birthday, leaving him and his five brothers to be reared by his Lutheran pastor father, Johann Froebel. Froebel's father tried, with little success, to teach young Friedrich. Often, little Friedrich's only solace was in the natural world outside of his boyhood home. He loved to play in the magnificent German countryside, which remained his source of inspiration for learning forevermore. Every blade of grass and every rock informed his sense of wonder and ignited his spirit of adventure. Each time that he held a rock in his hand, he would look at each aspect of the rock's formation and store the mental image for later use. Shapes, colors, and textures etched their way into his memory bank of the great outdoors, his best childhood classroom (Froebel, 1826/1885).

All of these early outdoor experiences became central to his use of play as a method of learning, and it's no wonder that Froebel is the first person to be credited with the term *playground* when, in 1826, he called for every town to have one, "Every town should have its own common playground for boys" (Froebel, 1826/1885, p. 114).

Froebel enhanced his confidence as a learner during his teen years, when he lived with his uncle and apprenticed as a forester, surveyor, and assessor. After some time, Froebel began his formal college work and emerged as a true scholar with interests in mineralogy, physics, natural history, chemistry, mathematics, and languages (Wolfe, 2002). While Froebel embraced the sciences and scholarly knowledge, he never forgot his religious teachings as the son of a Lutheran minister. For Froebel, science and religion could be in unity with each other and this concept remained with him throughout his entire life (Frost, 2010).

Despite an early interest in architecture, Froebel changed course to pursue a teaching career. In 1805, he accepted a position at the Frankfort Model School in a program that was inspired by the teachings of Pestalozzi. After two years, he left to work as a private tutor, but resumed his interest in Pestalozzi in 1808 when he was able to study directly under him (Brosterman, 1997). From this great master, Froebel learned the importance of "things before words" as a teaching philosophy, which he interpreted as the use of objects for enhancing comprehension. Later, in 1811, he enrolled in the University of Gottingen, where he studied chemistry, physics, mineralogy, and natural history (Wolfe, 2002).

As a patriotic citizen, Froebel served as a soldier in the War of 1812. After the war, he worked as an assistant in a museum in Berlin where he refined his knowledge about crystallography, and was offered a professorship of mineralogy in Stockholm, Sweden. However, he did not accept the position because he had decided to establish his own school in Keilhau, Germany (Brosterman, 1997).

The Keilhau School

In early nineteenth-century Germany, many students began attending school at the age of ten, so Froebel designed a program for this age group at Keilhau, in 1817. After several years, he ascertained that school should begin at a younger age because he felt that his students had much to unlearn. During his frequent walks in the hills adjacent to the school he began dreaming of his new vision of education for young children. He wanted it to be different than the rigid forms of schooling prevalent at that time for older children. Each day, as he walked to the top of the hill now known as Froebelick (Froebel's view), he tried to create a name for his educational dream. He believed that if he used the word *school*, it would just become a form of what was already in existence. One day, feeling inspired by the verdant countryside below his hilltop view, he coined the term *kindergarten*, to signify his new approach to early education as a children's garden for learning (Froebel, 1826/1885).

His Dream Takes Shape: Child-Centered Play

While at Keilhau, this learned mathematician, architect, and scholar built on his learning of the *objects before words* concept of his mentor, Pestalozzi. He began to formulate his own system of block play and became the first educator to incorporate *block play* as a method of learning for the school. In his book, *The Education of Man,* Froebel states,

> the best material for building representations is, at the beginning, a number of wooden blocks whose front surface is always one square inch, and whose length increases by inches from one to twelve. (Froebel, 1826/1885, p. 208)

Another key concept that Froebel developed at Keilhau was the notion of *child-centered play*, as he describes in the following passage:

> But the expression of a good, pure heart, a thoughtful, pure mind, is as it bears a unity in itself. . . . This eager desire is fulfilled to man in the stage of childhood by finding himself in complete possession of animated play; since he, by this play, is placed in the center of all things. (Froebel, 1826/1885, p. 59)

Ages and Stages

During his years at Keilhau and in the years that followed, Froebel was formulating a theory of developmental ages and stages much like Rousseau and Pestalozzi. Froebel determined that life could be divided into the stages of infancy, childhood, boyhood, and adulthood (Frost, 2010). While it may seem simple today, at that time, the rigidity of the schooling practices lacked any sense of the individual differences of children. Thus, Froebel's recognition of individual differences and developmental stages was a rare component in educational practices and, along with his concept of using play as a method of learning, these were considered to be radical concepts (Froebel, 1826/1885).

Kindergarten

In 1837, Froebel and his wife, Henriette, moved to Bad Blankenburg. Although she died in 1839, he continued to pursue his vision of a school for young children. In 1840, Froebel opened the first kindergarten in a yellow stucco building. The manifestation of his educational dream, which coincided with the four hundredth anniversary of the printing press, has been lauded as another major milestone for education. Today, the building houses a museum to honor Froebel and the birthplace of kindergarten (Moore, 2002a).

Once Froebel's garden for children, or kindergarten, commenced at Bad Blankenburg, the news of his system of a child-centered and play-based approach to schooling spread quickly across Germany, Europe, and, eventually, the rest of the world. Much of his success is attributed to the fact that he was able to articulate his theories about block play, sensory experiences, and the value of educational materials. In his kindergarten model of schooling, Froebel demonstrated how to educate students with carefully designed items that he labeled as *Gifts* that were offered to the children in a specific sequence (Froebel, 1904).

Not only did Froebel create a system of schooling, he also became known for his trainings for teachers who were interested in this new kindergarten concept. To prepare for these sessions, he took his blocks along with a miniature traveling set of the Gifts to use in his demonstrations. By doing so, he opened the door for women to become teachers. Froebel traveled throughout Germany and shared his expertise in trainings that emphasized the benefits of open-ended play with the blocks and other related materials. Prior to his kindergarten movement, blocks were not part of the traditional curriculum. As Norman Brosterman points out in *Inventing kindergarten,* Froebel introduced a new way of perceiving education and, as a result, blocks became one of the most important legacies of kindergarten (Brosterman, 1997).

While toys were popular in Europe, they were usually highly stylized, realistic, and so specific that they could be used for only one particular purpose. Even the blocks were limited because they were varied in shape and style, and most would not stack. Froebel introduced simpler blocks as a way of promoting open-ended play because he believed that knowledge must be acquired through active engagement in which children are free to see, touch, move, feel, and manipulate the materials. To promote the concept of using tangible objects to support learning, Froebel created a set of educational materials, which he called Gifts (Froebel, 1904).

Froebel's Gifts

The first group of objects to share with young children, Gift One, is a set of primary-colored yarn balls on strings. The colorful balls could be used in many ways such as dangling in front of a baby to encourage reaching, reinforcing the baby's grasp, helping a child learn to play catch, and using as a prop for storytelling activities. With the soft texture to encourage sensory play and bright colors that add visual appeal, the yarn balls serve as compelling objects that enhance development (Froebel, 1904).

Gift Two consists of a sphere, cylinder, and cube block suspended from a wooden rod. Children learn about the nature of each shape, as well as the similarities and differences between them. For instance, the cylinder has an unending rounded side like the sphere and yet has a flat side like the cube. For Froebel, the objects in Gift Two represent the unity of the world and the nature of God. Even today, Gift Two is the gift that is most commonly associated with Froebel and is incorporated into the signage of the kindergarten in Germany (Moore, 2002a).

The next gift in the series, Gift Three, is the first of the set of building blocks. It is a set of small cubes, which support open-ended constructive play. Children can manipulate the blocks to construct various objects such as a chair, sofa, or table. Afterward, they can take the structures apart and reassemble them into new structures. Due to the size and shape of the cubes in Gift Three, little hands can build, disassemble, and rebuild quickly, as soon as a new idea comes to mind (Froebel, 1904).

For Gifts Four through Six, Froebel continued with the theme of blocks and created sets of various sizes and shapes. Children can explore more complex play challenges with these sets and construct a variety of structures. Next, sets Seven through Nine add parquetry blocks, sticks, and rings to help students develop an understanding of lines and curves in the constructive process. For Gifts Nine through Eighteen, the Gifts feature grids, pin prick sewing, cutting, weaving, and folding. Gift Nineteen introduced the concepts of line and point with volume to allow the child to build free-standing structures (Froebel, 1904).

Over a century later, the esteemed architect, R. Buckminster Fuller remembered his work with the Gifts in kindergarten, and credited Gift Nineteen as one of the inspirations for his work. The Twentieth Gift was clay for modeling, which is a motivational tool that utilizes knowledge from the previous Gifts to create new objects in creative and artistic formations (Moore, 2002a).

Froebel instructed the teachers to use Gifts Two through Ten as materials to encourage the creation of new structures, noting that the open-ended aspect of blocks facilitates constructive play. Froebel's emphasis on mathematics is evidenced by the gradation of sizes and shapes, and he drew upon his early experiences with crystals as inspiration for the planes and contours of his learning materials (Moore, 2002a).

With access to the materials developed by Froebel, the child could become a constructive innovator, beginning in kindergarten. Anna Lloyd Wright implemented his methods and materials with her young son, who became the most celebrated architect of modern times. Later, Frank Lloyd Wright reminisced about his experiences with these educational tools and attributed his inspiration as an architect to Froebel's influence on his early development. The Frank Lloyd Wright Museum in Chicago features the Froebel Gifts on display and for sale (Moore, 2002a).

Finger Plays

Froebel's theory of play as pedagogy included instrumental music, songs, and finger plays. He recognized the educational value of fingerspielen, which is the German word for finger play, and elaborated on this language play genre by developing new variations. Froebel understood that this fun and fanciful form of play helps children learn numerical and linguistic concepts through stories and rhymes that provide active engagement. Finger plays are just one example of the ways that he used rhymes, rhythms, movement, and music to augment teaching in the kindergarten classroom. Froebel (1844/1895) wrote *Mother Play and Nursery Songs* as a resource for mothers and teachers of young children. Later, in 1878, Elizabeth Peabody translated the book into English for an American audience (Peabody, 1878).

A GARDEN FOR KINDERGARTEN

In the book, *The Education of Man,* Froebel emphasized that play is of the utmost importance: "play at this time is not trivial, it is highly serious and of deep significance" (Froebel,1826/1885, p. 55). Froebel strived to provide open-ended experiences for the learner and believed that imaginative play is important for all aspects of the child's development. His playful methods included blocks, finger plays, drawing, cutting, weaving, folding, music, and movement as well as adventures outdoors. In his garden at Keilhau, he provided space for a community garden as well as a plot for each individual child to cultivate. Froebel believed that gardens are essential because they nurture both social and spiritual development. Over time, all of the schools that adhered to the Froebel philosophy added gardens to their grounds and to the curriculum (Froebel,1826/1885).

Play Fest

Froebel advocated for outdoor free play by organizing a special play festival at Altenstein Park in 1851. He sponsored this event to encourage children from the community to celebrate play. It was a forerunner to today's popular Play Days and the community has continued the tradition. One memory from that day is celebrated in the following song:

> As the flowers in the garden blow
> So, we in kindergarten grow
> And with our glances bright
> Our gardener delights! (Froebel, 1904)

Essence of Play

For Froebel, play was central to all child development and children's rights. In the following passage, Froebel captures the essence of play:

> Play is the purest, most spiritual activity of man at this stage and, at the same time, typical of human life as a whole—of the inner hidden natural life in man and all things. It gives, therefore, joy, freedom, contentment, inner and outer rest, peace with the world. It holds the sources of all that is good. (Froebel, 1826/1885, p. 55)

Seemingly, no other quote elevates play to the same extent as these words. A contemporary educational historian, Jennifer Wolfe, suggests that Froebel had a remarkable understanding of children and their childhood need for play (Wolfe, 2002).

Monuments to Play

Once misunderstood and even ridiculed as an old fool who plays with children, Froebel lived to see his philosophy honored and his kindergarten model implemented in Germany and throughout Europe. Later, his teachings encircled the globe and his birthday, April 21st, is celebrated as International Kindergarten Day. Additionally, several monuments honor his memory in Germany. The most notable monument is located in eastern Germany, at Froebelick. It is an enormous stone structure that was erected to portray Froebel's Gift Two. Below the monument is a marker, which designates the site as the place where Froebel created his dream for kindergarten (Moore, 2002b).

When Froebel died, in 1852, his first resting place was Froebelsruh in Schweina, Germany, and his grave marker was created by Ernst Luther, the grandson of Martin Luther. On his one hundredth birthday, in 1882, his remains were moved to a more prominent grave, also in Schweina. Froebel is buried on a hillside and his gravestone is adorned with Gift Two, the sphere, cylinder, and cube (Moore, 2002b). The inscription on the gravestone reads,

> "Come let us live for our children."
> Friedrich Froebel
> Born April 21, 1782
> Died June 21, 1852
> At Marienthal
> The great friend of childhood and man
> From his grateful admirers
> 1 Corinthians 13:8

CONCLUSION

As parents, educators, community members, play leaders, play professionals, and the world come together to celebrate the child's right to play, let us remember Friedrich Froebel who championed the right to play and playing to learn, thus laying a permanent cornerstone of child-centered play for us to emulate. Certainly, Froebel admonishes us to accept that play is the highest form of child development and he advises us to cultivate it. We can learn from his legacy and adopt his motto, " Come let us live for our children." (Froebel, 1826/1885, p. 89). We can build creative opportunities for play, inclusive and imaginative playgrounds as new monuments to play, and support active engagement, whether at home, in the classroom, outdoors, or wherever children find themselves.

REFERENCES

Brosterman, N. (1997). *Inventing kindergarten.* Harry N. Abrams, Publishers.

Froebel, F. (1826, 1885). *The education of man.* Translated by J. Jarvis. A. Lovell & Company.

Froebel, F. (1844/1895). *Mother play and nursery songs.* Lee & Shepard.

Froebel, F. (1904). *Third and last volume of Friedrich Froebel's pedagogics of the kindergarten.* (J. Jarvis, Trans.) Woodward & Tieman Company.

Frost, J. (2010) *A history of children's play and play environments: Toward a contemporary child-saving movement.* Routledge.

Moore, M. R. (2002a). An American's journey to kindergarten's birthplace. *Childhood Education, 79*, 1, 15–20.

Moore, M. R. (2002b). Keilhau, an important Froebel destination. www.friedrichfroebel.com/keilhau/moore.html.

Peabody, E. (Ed.) (1878). *Mother play and nursery songs by Froebel.* Lathrop.

Wolfe, J. (2002). *Learning from the past: Historical voices in early childhood education, 2nd Edition.* Piney Branch Press.

2

John Dewey

1859–1952

LaDonna Atkins

John Dewey.

> *In play activity, it is said, the interest is in the activity for its own sake; in work it is in the product or result in which the activity terminates. Hence the former is purely free, while the latter is tied down by the end to be achieved.* (Dewey, 1910, p. 164)

John Dewey was a renowned psychologist, political activist, educator, philosopher, and play scholar. His contributions to educational thinking and the purposes of play are still relevant and studied today. John Dewey was an educational pioneer and paved the way for play to be seen as an important part of pedagogy and influential to children's growth. Dewey believed that education begins with play and that play results in thinking and reflection, which in turn becomes the basis for work. These ideals continue to frame learning and childhood today (Lindsay, 2016). Dewey's passion for educating people of all demographics was a vital protocol that set a precedent for American education. The contributions of John Dewey and the attention to his work, theories, and practices continue to impact education in modern society.

PRAGMATIC PHILOSOPHER

Dewey was best known as a pragmatic philosopher and an educational reformer whose impact transformed education and forever changed thoughts on child play. In fact, he published hundreds of documents and articles that directly challenged the idea that knowledge is primarily theoretical. His contributions to society include developing a metaphysical theory that examined human nature. According to Dewey, metaphysics is a modern philosophy that favors a naturalistic approach. He viewed knowledge as arising from an active application of the human organism to its environment (Field, n.d.). Dewey also practiced as a pragmatic philosopher in that he encouraged and practiced experimental inquiry. He developed a version of pragmatism called instrumentalism, which is a perspective that requires active inquiry and participation that results in ideas (Alexander & Hickman, 1998).

While instrumentalism was one of Dewey's more significant contributions, it should be noted that Dewey also contributed to the concept of democracy, pioneered functional psychology, and was the leader of the progressive movement in education. His influence on democracy, the image of the child, and his theories of active learning transformed education. In examining the work of John Dewey, the essential impacts to be examined in this chapter include his ideologies on play/playfulness, the role of play in education, and his influence that led other play scholars to research and support this natural phenomena (Alexander & Hickman, 1998).

Ideologies of Play

The central premise of educational play and other early childhood theories was influenced by the work of John Dewey. Dewey changed societal thinking and ideas of children with his research (Platz and Arellano, 2011). He advocated for a more natural approach to learning which emphasized social interaction and experiential learning. Dewey's educational ideas were built upon many philosophies of his time as well as the work of Friedrich Froebel. Dewey commended Froebel's work on kindergarten and play, but opposed other ideologies. For example, Dewey challenged Froebel's practices of elaborate symbolism (Beatty, 2017).

Froebelian principles were initially based on an absolute and finite logical framework, which was in direct opposition to Dewey's principles. In effect, when Froebel perceived the notion of a game, he believed that childhood could be interpreted in the educational work of playing a game. Alternatively, Dewey did not believe play was only an external activity; he saw play as an internal process, not dependent upon the involvement of games (Dewey, 1910).

According to Dewey,

> The more unfitted the physical object for its imagined purpose, such as a cube for a boat, the greater the supposed appeal to the imagination. (Dewey, 1910, p. 166)

Thus, Dewey believed that the more mundane the object, the more imagination needed to transform the object. Although Dewey thought highly of Froebel's work, he "found inconsistencies between [Froebel's] theory and [Froebel's] practice and criticized him for his complete formula of development" (Dewey & Dewey, 1962, p. 77). In sum, Dewey believed that no formula could completely define childhood.

Dewey did agree with Froebel's ideas on individual-directed activity. However, Dewey emphasized more of a need for freedom, personal interest, and real-life opportunities. Froebel's central elements of his philosophy were the development of spiritual harmony and nature (Platz & Arellano, 2011).

Developed in an era known for diversity and poverty, Dewey's philosophy emphasized the importance of considering the child's community and adherence to a democratic model (Dewey, 1916). Froebel and Dewey had opinions, hypotheses, and theories about children and their potential: the meaning of children's work, and the meaning of children's play, and made significant contributions to the field of play in education. Finally, both Dewey's and Froebel's works theorized that children are active learners who need opportunities to investigate and experience life. These premises for investigation in children eventually would grow into adult work (Tanner, 1997).

The works of Dewey and Froebel contributed to contemporary theories about childhood education. These childhood education theories have evolved, and thus, the benefits of Dewey and Froebel's research about play will continue to be essential to the basis of research about education and development. Dewey's rejection of the Froebelian thought model spawned the debate of play and its role in education. The controversies brought the topic of play to the forefront of educational discussion. Therefore, Dewey's thoughts and ideas were instrumental in developing support for the richness and importance of play (Beatty, 2017).

Dewey believed that as children grew, so did their process of thinking (Dewey, 1916). He viewed education as a lifetime process. Before ideas about constructivism were well known, Dewey wrote that children needed to be involved in their learning environment. He supported learning that wove together home and community (Dewey, 1913).

Dewey also challenged behaviorist theories that emphasized passive learning and favored a natural learning environment. He described play as

> "a name given to those activities which are not consciously performed for the sake of any result beyond themselves; activities which are enjoyable in their execution without reference for ulterior purpose" (Dewey, 1913, p. 725). He believed children could be independent, capable learners at young ages and that their interests and familiarity were the key to engagement (Dewey, 1916).

Dewey found that play gradually evolves into work and conscious intention, which supports the role of play in education. As a result of his influence, educational theorists and teachers view free play and educational play as beneficial for children's development. Dewey explained that play develops into work as children age into adults. Therefore, time for play in childhood can lead to a successful adulthood (Dennis, 1970).

Role of Play in Education

"Education is not preparation for life; education is life itself" (John Dewey, 1916, p. 239). John Dewey advocated for play in education and believed that educators should create an environment to support play. He believed that each child had potential and power within and, given the opportunity to play, along with the appropriate materials, a child could reach its potential. As children play, they begin to look for more visible achievement. Dewey asserted that concepts are formed and transformed by experience, reflection, and activity (Dennis, 1970).

It is worth noting that Dewey saw classrooms as miniature civilizations in which children interact and develop a moral compass (Tanner, 1997). Through this lens, play can be seen as innovative in process and nature. He proposed that when children engage in problem-solving processes, they learn by posing questions and investigating daily problems. In this model, teachers perceive play as inventive and create learning opportunities (Dewey & Dewey, 1962).

Dewey's ideals were centered around growth of character in the following three ways: every child has work to do within the community, the teachers model concern for each child, and discipline is generative rather than restrictive. Discipline issues are redirected toward positive behaviors, and children are expected to work through problems (Tanner, 1997). In Dewey's model, education should be focused on developing good habits, fostering creativity, facilitating innovation, and promoting inventiveness. The teacher's role is to provide support, thus spurring growth within the classroom (Dewey, et al, 1916).

In sum, John Dewey supported the notion of play because it prepares a child to enter society by fostering a solid moral character and strong work ethic. Dewey championed play because it can lead to real and conceptual learning (Tanner, 1997). Investigative play is aimed at learning the skills of inquiry and learning how to relate cause and effect (Beatty, 2017).

Thoughts on Playfulness

> *Playfulness is a more important consideration than play. The former is an attitude of mind; the latter is a passing outward manifestation of this attitude. When things are treated simply as vehicles of suggestion, what is suggest overrides the thing. Hence the playful attitude is one of freedom Dewey.* (1910, p. 162)

John Dewey supported the spirit of play and wrote about the concept of playfulness in his book *How We Think*. He defined playfulness as the spirit that embraces play; "Hence the playful attitude is one of freedom" (Dewey, 1910, p. 162). Dewey promoted the idea that playfulness is relative to freedom and joy. In fact, Dewey often expressed that using play in learning had psychological and intellectual benefits. Dewey said, "To be playful and serious at the same time is possible, and it defines the ideal mental condition" (Dewey, 1910, p. 218).

Dewey supported active engagement because it facilitates creativity. He described how playfulness can lead to free mental play and pretend play can lead to meaningful representation in young children. For example, "When the child plays horse with a broom and cars with chairs, the fact that the broom does not really represent a horse, or a chair a locomotive, is of no account" (Dewey, 1910, p. 162). Dewey described this engagement as: "A play and a story blend insensibly into each other" (Dewey, 1910, p. 162). Dewey further explained that natural play opportunities arise which may support children's conceptual development and eventually lead to them becoming more successful adults (Dewey, 1910).

Dewey theorized that playfulness had value in childhood and adulthood and supported a more playful approach to education. He believed that playfulness offers the possibility of bringing more joy into the realm of teaching and learning (Platz & Arellano, 2011).

Influence on Play

> *Dewey "opened spaces for others to make personal connections between his philosophies and their own."* (Richards, 2012, p. 41)

The study of play in itself is historical, and has been researched by many scholars who advocate for play. Dewey inspired many educators to study play in order to comprehend the intricacies of human nature. Many play scholars have used his philosophies to develop their own ideologies of play, which may or may not be reflective of his true vision. However, Dewey would support the creation of new ideologies. He established a laboratory school for scholars to continue to study pedagogy and his ideas radically challenged traditional educational beliefs and generated an educational study movement (Richards, 2012).

John Dewey's influence on the study of play has been significant. However, even though many well known play scholars credit Dewey in the development of their own philosophies, others believe his description of play was too vague (Frost, Wortham & Reifel, 2012).

CONCLUSION

Dewey expressed his support of play and experiential learning, which led to educational reform and inspired countless research studies. He explained that a playful attitude could bring about vocational advancement through perceptual environments, and his philosophies and pedagogical guidance resulted in educational practices to support play (Dewey et al., 1916). As his influence spread throughout the United States and other countries, John Dewey challenged researchers to study play and to explore innovative models of thinking about pedagogy.

REFERENCES

Alexander, T., & Hickman, L. (1998). *The essential Dewey, Volume 2.* Indiana University Press.

Beatty, B. (2017). John Dewey high hopes for play: Democracy and education and progressive era controversies over play in kindergarten and preschool education. *The Journal of the Gilded Age and Progressive Era, 16*, 4, 424–437.

Dennis, L. (1970). Play in Dewey's theory of education. *Young Children, 25*, 4, 230–235. doi:10.2307/3332028.

Dewey, J. (1910). *How we think.* Heath.

Dewey, J. (1913). *Interest and effort in education.* Houghton, Mifflin and Company.

Dewey, J. (1916). *Democracy and education.* Courier Corporation.

Dewey, J., Baysinger, P. R., Boydston, J. A., Hook, S., & Levine, B. (1916). *Democracy and education.* Southern Illinois University Press. Dewey Studies: Resources for Scholars. (2016). Retrieved February 5, 2018 from http://www.johndeweysociety.org/dewey-studies/resources-for-scholars.

Dewey, J., & Dewey, E. (1962). *Schools of tomorrow.* Dutton & Co.

Field, R. (n.d.). Internet encyclopedia of philosophy: John Dewey. Retrieved May 28, 2018 from https://www.iep.utm.edu/dewey/.

Lindsay, G. (2016). John Dewey and Reggio Emilia: Worlds apart—one vision. *Australian Art Education, 37*, 21–37.

Platz, D., & Arellano, J. (2011). Time tested early childhood theories and practices. *Education, 132*, 1, 54–63.

Richards, R. (2012). *Young children's art experiences: A visual ethnographic study with four children in their homes, early childhood centre and schools.* Doctoral Thesis, University of New England, Armidale. https://epublications.une.edu.au/vital/access/manager/Repository/une:11597.

Tanner, L. (1997). *Dewey's laboratory school: Lessons for today.* Teachers College Press.

3

Maria Montessori

1870–1952

Josh Thompson

Maria Montessori.

Play is the avenue for children to perform their greatest feat, to construct themselves as human beings.

Maria Montessori saw the child as she is, acting on her world in a playful spirit. Play, to Montessori, became the avenue for the child to perform her greatest feat, to construct the human being. Trained as a physician, Montessori utilized her expertise to *diagnose the pathology* of childhood, and prescribe a cure (Montessori, 1949/1995). The problem exists not in the child, but in us, in the environment, in the schooling, and in the constant interruption of the flow of development and concentration, which the young child brings to her aid and assistance when she plays. And all of this Montessori wrote about over a hundred years ago (Montessori, 1912/1964). If only we would listen, if only we could hear.

MONTESSORI AS HUMANIST

As a humanist, Montessori believed in the power of the individual, the "home" of the soul, a life force that rises up within the human to direct and construct the best version of the Self (Montessori, 1949/1995). This life force often exists below the surface, suppressed by conformity, rules, and schooling. But it exists in all living forms.

A true scientist, Montessori (1912/1964) demonstrated the power of work and play, of concentration and focus, on the child's construction of her whole Self, and she replicated her educational experience over and over, first in Italy, and then throughout the world. A future adult version of a true Self was definitely the eventual outcome of a childhood well lived, but that final product was not the intent or purpose of childhood. The child has her very being in the present, not in doing something now so the future Self can become a certain way, or perform a specific task, or get this or that kind of job.

The child is not a widget being made in a factory nor a blank slate to be written upon. The child is constructing her Self now, in the present, in this very place. Play and work, concentration and focus, are tools with which the child lives, and comes fully alive, in the here and now (Hyde, 2011; Hymes, 1965). This is the very substance of which the ancient wisdom writer speaks: "Unless you become like a little child, you cannot enter the kingdom of heaven" (Matthew 18:3). Montessori's own biographer, E. M. Standing, drew the connection between work and play in Montessori classrooms: "he loves it, lives it, rejoices in it, perseveres in it, repeats it—*because it is the means by which he is perfecting himself*" (Standing 1962, p. 145; italics original).

Montessori wrote extensively, superbly, though much of her text is wrapped in profuse obscurity. Patience and the mindset of the child as the source and revealer of her true nature, work together to provide the reader with ample tools to dig deep, and abide there, in Montessori's own words about work and play:

> Does Nature make a difference between work and play or occupation and rest? Watch the unending activity of the flowing stream or the growing tree. See the breakers of the ocean, the unceasing movements of the earth, the planets, the sun and the stars. All creation is life, movement, work. What about our hearts, our lungs, our bloodstream which work continuously from birth till death? Have they asked for some rest? Not even during sleep are they inactive. What about our mind which works without intermission while we are awake or asleep? (Montessori, 1961, p. 138)

Prepared Environment

The fundamentals of playful learning identified by Hirsh-Pasek and associates (2009) and Fisher and colleagues (2010) indicate that Montessori principles align well with these elements:

> Montessori schools are known for creating classrooms in which children choose from a number of playful, hands-on activities that have been prearranged by adults who serve as guides rather than directors of education. Importantly, the children might not even know that there was a learning goal in mind. (Hirsh-Pasek, 2009, p. 45)

Role of the Teacher

Montessori prescribed for us a role, not to teach the child but to assist the enormous internal forces of childhood and to reduce the impediments to development. Montessori told us how to get out of the way, how to enter into the world the child is creating through scientific observation. Our role is to observe, not as a passive, uninvolved bystander, but as a collaborator, a co-conspirator in the work the child has undertaken, to be fully human. The work of the teacher (Montessori called us Directors) is less about filling the empty vessel of the child with a pre-scripted curriculum, but more about watching the child. Through astute, trained observation, the Director notes the child's actions, her eyes and focus, her hands and their movement, the motion and energy she brings to her work. The Director must understand how to reduce impediments and increase engagement with the materials (Montessori, 1947).

> An ordinary teacher cannot be transformed into a Montessori teacher, but must be created anew, having rid herself of pedagogical prejudices. The first step is self-preparation of the imagination, for the Montessori teacher has to visualize a child who is not yet there, materially speaking, and must have faith in the child who will reveal himself through work. The different types of deviated children do not shake the faith of this teacher, who sees a different type of child in the spiritual field, and looks confidently for this Self to show when attracted by work that interests. She waits for the children to show signs of concentration. (Montessori, 1947, p. 67)

Curriculum

The classical Montessori program provides a set of prescribed curriculum materials for each class (AMS, 2020). The materials have been crafted through trial and error to optimize the child's engagement and experience in constructing the Self. The pink tower ironically represents the beautiful prepared materials (Figure 3.1). The direct purpose for sensorial materials in the Primary Class (3, 4, 5, and 6-year-olds) focuses on visual discrimination, coordination of gross and fine motor movements, and increasing precision (Montessori, 1949/1995).

Pink Tower. ***Photo courtesy of Nienhuis.***

Indirectly, the child is storing away impressions, what Montessori called *mnemes* (Montessori, 1949/1995), in preparation for future understanding of cubed roots in algebra. The smallest cube is 1 cm high by 1 cm long by 1 cm wide. The successive cubes increase in volume proportionally until the largest is 10 cm by 10 cm by 10 cm, cubed. Next, this experiential encounter with the Base-10 number system is replicated throughout the classroom, as it is the one, among all the numeration and counting systems, that is the most prolific in our human culture (Montessori, 1912/1964).

Montessori designed these scientifically prepared lessons with the intent of providing specialized experience with abstract concepts that later would be activated through labels and language, with explicit detail. But for now, during the sensorial period of development, the child need only encounter, manipulate, visually discriminate, and return the material to the shelf for future use. The prominence of the constructed tower in its place in the classroom becomes a beacon, a lighthouse, calling out to the child, "Remember when . . . ", and evoking in the child, "Come again . . .", the future dimensions of study and understanding yet to be explored. The control of error is inherent in the work. It doesn't take a teacher with a red pen to mark upon the child's work, either in the affirmative or negative, that the child has succeeded in all the dimensions of this task. The child is doing the work, and able to evaluate the results within her own schema. Of course, the trained observer may comment on points of perfection, drawing the child's attention to the finer details of work. But it is not the adult who is the arbiter of success but the child herself. As Montessori explained,

> This is education, understood as a help to life; an education from birth, which feeds a peaceful revolution and unites all in a common aim, attracting them as to a single centre. Mothers, fathers, politicians: all must combine in their respect and help for this delicate work of formation, which the little child carries on in the depth of a profound psychological mystery, under the tutelage of an inner guide. This is the bright new hope for mankind. (Montessori, 1949/1995, p. 15)

Integration

The domains of development exist within the whole child. Montessori's approach to work and play integrates the whole of development, aiming with precision at each explicit domain as if that realm were the only one in play, but always in context of the whole of development. This persistent attention to the integration of faculties highlights her genius, wrought through scientific observation. She noticed that the child craves intense concentration, and will act out if impeded or distracted from that deep level of engagement.

> We ourselves have lost this deep and vital sensitiveness, and in the presence of children in whom we see it reviving, we feel as if we were watching a mystery being unfolded. It shows itself in the delicate act of free choice, which a teacher untrained in observation can trample on before she even discerns it, much as an elephant tramples the budding flower about to blossom in its path.
>
> The child whose attention has once been held by a chosen object, while he concentrates his whole self on the repetition of the exercise, is a delivered soul in the sense of the spiritual safety of which we speak. From this moment there is no need to worry about him—except to prepare an environment which satisfies his needs, and to remove obstacles which may bar his way to perfection. (Montessori, 1949/1995, p. 248)

The work is connecting the whole child, spirit, soul, mind, and strength, through integration of these emerging faculties. The child's use of the hand, to touch and feel, to stroke and discriminate, to move and manipulate objects, is in fact moving his brain. He sees objects and perceives Self in the interaction and manipulation (Montessori, 1949/1995).

Only recently has brain research validated what Montessori discovered about the work of the hand on the construction of the brain. Patricia Kuhl, University of Washington, describes many facets of brain development discovered under the magnetoencephalography (MEG) machine, which provides real-time functional images of brain activity (Kuhl, 2010).

The coordination of the primary motor cortex and Broca's area typically governing speech indicates that the infant child anticipates speech, evokes it even from responsive caregivers. This initiation of playful learning in the very young child was recognized and accounted for in Montessori's design of meaningful learning environments. She planned for choice, initiation, and concentration in her classrooms and through intense training of directors in the arts and skills of focused observation. She wrote, "the entire Montessori method is based on the spontaneous activity of the child which is aroused precisely by the interest the child takes in the material" (Montessori, 1995, p. 14).

Angeline Lillard (2013) further explores this dimension of playful learning. She aligns principles of playful learning with Montessori ideals. Seven dimensions align between the two: both provide overall structure, involve objects and lessons, collaboration with peers is possible, intrinsic motivation is cultivated, and fun is involved. For purposes here, the principle of free choice needs deliberation to better understand how the Montessori theory promotes playful learning.

> With playful learning, children's own interests drive the agenda. An adult provides the activities and objects and guides the children's engagement with the materials, but an aura of free choice pervades. Important to this aura in playful learning, no one forces children to engage if they choose not to do so. If children choose to engage in some way other than expected, the adult follows the children's lead and tries imperceptibly to return the youngsters to the learning agenda. Choice in Montessori education varies by level. Free choice exists at the macro-level of classroom environment: most of the time, most Montessori students choose what they work on. A child might decide to iron napkins, cut carrots and offer them around the classroom, wash a table, or take apart and put back together a puzzle map of Europe. . . . At the more micro-level of exercises within the environment, Montessori education offers less freedom. (Lillard, 2013, pp. 165–166)

What's Normal Anyway? The Child as Leader in Play

With the end in sight, the fulfillment of her childish dreams and aspirations for total independence, the young child immerses herself in her work. The Montessori classroom, looking all stark and bare, doesn't appear to be "fun" or "entertaining." Yet, the child here engages herself playfully in "work" that feeds her soul's craving, satisfies her highest need, to become her true Self. Dorer (2018) lists four goals for the primary aged (3-6 years old) as matched with the Practical Life materials:

> It is important to emphasize that Practical Life, while it appears to focus on a variety of skills, actually has just 4 essential goals. Those goals are:
>
> - the development and refinement of a *sense of order*,
> - the encouragement and growth of *concentration*,
> - *coordination of movement* involving both large and small muscles, and
> - most important to this discussion, the development of *independence.* (p. 42, emphasis original)

CONCLUSION

This work of independence comes down to the concept, to paraphrase Montessori—*If I've done my job right, the children don't need me—This is the child at play, creating her Self, her best version of Self.* This is what is normal, anyway.

REFERENCES

American Montessori Society (AMS). (2020). *Classroom materials*. Available online at https://amshq.org/About-Montessori/Inside-the-Montessori-Classroom/Early-Childhood#montessori-learning-materials.

Dorer, M. (2018). Independence: A Montessori journey. *Montessori life, 30*, 1, pp. 40–45.

Fisher, K., Hirsh-Pasek, K., Golinkoff, R., Singer, D., & Berk, L.W. (2010). Playing around in school: Implications for learning and education policy. In *The Oxford handbook of the development of play*, edited by Anthony D. Pellegrini, pp. 341–362. Oxford University Press.

Hirsh-Pasek, K., Golinkoff, R. M., Berk, L., & Singer, D. (2009). *A mandate for playful learning in preschool: Applying the scientific evidence*. Oxford University Press.

Hyde, B. (2011). Montessori and Jerome W. Berryman: Work, play, religious education and the art of using the Christian language system. *British journal of religious education, 33*(3), pp. 341–353.

Hymes, J. L. (1965). Montessori. *Educational leadership, 23*, 3, pp. 127–131.

Kuhl, P. K. (2010). Brain mechanisms in early language acquisition. *Neuron, 67*, 5, pp. 713–727.

Lillard, A. S. (2013). Playful learning and Montessori education. *American journal of play, 5*, 2, pp. 157–186.

Montessori, Maria. (1912/1964). *The Montessori method: Scientific pedagogy as applied to child education in "The Children's Houses" with additions and revisions by the author* (translated from the Italian by Anne E. George). Robert Bentley, Inc.

Montessori, Maria. (1947). *Education for a new world*. Clio Press Ltd.

Montessori, Maria. (1949/1995). *The absorbent mind* (translated from the Italian by Claude A. Claremont, 1958). Henry Holt and Company.

Montessori, Maria. (1961). *What you should know about your child*. Kalakshetra Publications.

Montessori, Maria. (1995). Some words of advice to teachers. *AMI Communications, 4*,14, p. 4.

Standing, E.M. (1962). *Maria Montessori: Her life and work*. Mentor.

4

Johan Huizinga

1872–1945

Vivien L. Geneser and David J. Akpata

Johan Huizinga.

All play means something.

The Dutch historian, Johan Huizinga, illuminated both the beauty and foibles of mankind in his popular treatises. As a professor of history in Europe during the first half of the twentieth century, he integrated art, music, drama, and literature into his work, which was a departure from the prevailing nationalistic approach to teaching history at that time. Huizinga (1938) identified himself as a cultural historian and wrote *Homo Ludens: A Study of the Play-Element in Culture* to communicate his theory of play (Anchor, 1978; Colie, 1964). Originally published in Dutch, the book was already well established as a classic for scholars of play in the 1960s, but it has gained even more popularity since then as a resource for designers of digital media games who study gamification (Midgley, 2015; Peters & Simons, 1999; Salen & Zimmerman, 2003).

HUIZINGA AS CULTURAL HISTORIAN

Johan Huizinga expressed his appreciation for aesthetics with thorough descriptions and vibrant narratives during his lectures at Leiden, and in his publications. He was a dynamic professor who dared to amplify cultural topics when teaching college history. The ideas that Huizinga set forth in his books, such as *The Autumn of the Middle Ages, Men and Ideas (1919), Erasmus and the Age of Reformation (1924),* and *Homo Ludens: A Study of the Play-Element in Culture (1938)* continue to spark debates in academic meetings and journals. Huizinga was outspoken with his political beliefs and addressed his antiwar ideology and concern for journalistic freedom in local publications. Unfortunately, his views were deemed controversial and Huizinga was arrested for insubordination and imprisoned by the Nazis from 1941-1942. Johan Huizinga died in 1945 (Anchor, 1978; Colie, 1964; Midgely, 2015).

Play in Culture

Johan Huizinga (1938) offered a comprehensive explanation of play in *Homo Ludens: A Study of the Play-Element in Culture*. Beginning with the title, *Homo Ludens,* which roughly translates as "Man, the Player," homo represents *man* and ludens, which is the cognate of *ludes,* or ludicrous, refers to sport, play, and fun, he elaborates on the concept of play (Salen & Zimmerman, 2003). Huizinga defined play as a central activity, the primary formative element of human culture, and emphasized that playful activities represent the play element *of* culture rather than *in* culture" (Anchor, 1978). In his essay, "The Task of the Cultural Historian," Huizinga emphasized the importance of studying culture because "only when the scholar turns to determining the patterns of life, art, and thought taken all together can there actually be a be a question of cultural history" (Anchor, 1978, p. 65).

Huizinga (1938) acknowledged the ethereal quality of play with the statement,

> Play is a function of living but it is not susceptible of exact definition either logically, biologically, or aesthetically . . . the play-concept remains distinct from all other forms of thought in which we express the structure of mental and social life. (p. 6)

In other words, play is a free activity standing quite consciously outside *ordinary* life as being *not serious*, but at the same time absorbing the player intensely and utterly. Furthermore, Huizinga (1938) communicates the primordial essence of play, that it is fun for both humans and animals when he says, "Play is older than culture, for culture, however inadequately defined, always presupposes human society, and animals have not waited for man to teach them their playing" (p. 1).

Significance of Play

Huizinga asserted that play is not a trivial subject. As readers delve into *Homo Ludens*, they will begin to grasp his belief in the significance of play and to acknowledge that features of play are pervasive in every aspect of civilization. In his words:

> Real civilization cannot exist in the absence of a certain play-element, for civilization presupposes limitation and mastery of the self, the ability not to confuse its own tendencies with the ultimate and highest goal, but to understand that it is enclosed within certain bounds freely accepted. (Huizinga, 1938, p. 211)

Huizinga was not the only theorist to examine the unique and dynamic role of play in human development, but he was the first to offer an in-depth look at the functions of play in all aspects of the human experience (Anchor, 1978; Edwards, 2013). For example, in *Homo Ludens,* Huizinga (1938) highlights the importance of play by describing his observations of common patterns in how play is designated and expressed in a variety of languages (p. 29). He theorized that since every culture and language lists one or more words for play, it must have a cross-cultural, universal significance (Holst, 2017).

Huizinga (1938) states, "For many years the conviction has grown upon me that civilization arises and unfolds in and as play" (p. xi). Additionally, Huizinga (1938) emphasizes the universality of play when he says,

> The incidence of play is not associated with any particular stage of civilization or view of the universe. Any thinking person can see at a glance that play is a thing on its own, even if his language possesses no general concept to express it. Play cannot be denied. You can deny, if you like, nearly all abstractions: justice, beauty, truth, goodness, mind, God. You can deny seriousness, but not play. (p. 3)

Huizinga (1938) was fascinated by the role of apparel as an influence on behavior and he wrote about the impact of clothing, costumes, and wigs on play since dramatic accessories enable the wearer to transform into another being, "a stepping out of common reality into a higher order" (p.13). In the child's imagination, they believe they are "making an image of something different, something more beautiful, or more sublime, or more dangerous than what he usually is" (Huizinga, 1938, p. 14).

Peters & Simons (1999) discuss his appreciation for mirth and penchant for gaiety, since, after all, he wrote his doctoral dissertation on the figure of court jesters in Sanskrit dramatic literature (p. 591). Speaking of Western Civilization in *Homo Ludens,* Huizinga (1938) lamented the decline of formal attire, saying, "There is no more striking symptom of the decline of the play-factor than the disappearance of everything imaginative, fanciful, fantastic from men's dress after the French Revolution" (p. 192).

Characteristics of Play

Huizinga differentiated between the Greek concept of *paideia,* which refers to lighthearted child's play and *agon,* which pertains to sports. To Huizinga (1938), play could be described as having five main characteristics; 1) play is free, or voluntary 2) play is not ordinary or real life, 3) play is distinct from ordinary life as to locality and duration, 4) play creates order, and 5) play is connected with no material interest and no profit can be gained from it (p.13).

Play is free or voluntary. Free play is an intrinsically motivated behavior that is usually unscripted, open-ended, and involves spontaneous pursuits. It contrasts with activities that are necessary to survival, yet Huizinga postulates that it is essential to healthy development. Free play is a self-selected, freely chosen activity that is accompanied by feelings of joy, and a sense of transcendence from ordinary life. Thus, "child and animal play because they enjoy playing, and therein precisely lies their freedom" (Huizinga, 1938, p. 8).

Play is not ordinary or real life. Play involves rules but they are often different from ordinary life and may be fluid and ever-changing, depending on the players who are absorbed in the intensity of the moment. However, play makes sense to the player and even the most primitive forms of play, such as two dogs roughhousing, indicates an intuitive mutual understanding, since they do not injure each other. They share a reciprocal awareness that the play activity is pretense, make-believe (Rodriguez, 2006). As players engage in the playful activity, they are aware that their actions are in a different mental world and, to stay in the game, they must abide by rules. Huizinga (1938) explains, "These rules in their turn are a very important factor in the play-concept. All play has its rules. They determine what 'holds' in the temporary world circumscribed by play" (p. 9).

Play is distinct from ordinary life as to locality and duration. Play occurs within fixed boundaries and the players share a "magic circle" of activity (Huizinga, 1938). Within the bounds of this dimension, the players adhere to the playful shared consciousness. Whether the magic circle is located within the playground, the courtroom, or in a religious setting, the activities occur as a temporary world within the real world as a consecrated spot (Rodriguez, 2006). The player submits to the game with its rules, norms, and behaviors. The participants' culture shapes the expectations for the event and will also influence the subsequent memory of it (Salen & Zimmerman, 2003). Gadamer (2004) notes how boundaries can be flexible and observes that when spectators join in as participants, they become part of the play's flow (p.108).

Play creates order. Play has another positive feature in that it creates a sense of order. Huizinga (1938) asserts, "Inside the playground, an absolute and peculiar order reigns" and, when humans are engaged in activities, "play casts a spell over us; it is enchanting, captivating. It is invested in the noblest qualities we are capable of perceiving in things: rhythm and harmony" (p. 10). Additionally, Holst (2017) observes, "The more play seizes the players, the less aware they are of what they are playing" (p. 93).

Play is connected with no material interest and no profit can be gained from it. Strictly speaking, play is non-purposeful and the playing is subservient to material interests. Huizinga (1938) elaborates,

> Summing up the formal characteristic of play, we might call it a free activity standing quite consciously outside "ordinary" life as being "not serious" but at the same time absorbing the player intensely and utterly. It is an activity connected with no material interest, and no profit can be gained by it. It proceeds within its own proper boundaries of time and space according to fixed rules and in an orderly manner. It promotes the formation of social groupings that tend to surround themselves with secrecy and to stress the difference from the common world by disguise or other means. (p. 12)

Learning through play

Guiding students toward learning objectives by utilizing playful activities is not as pure and unrestricted as spontaneous "free play" but, within the bounds of a conceptual framework, a play-based curriculum can provide students with many of the benefits of play. Teaching with a playful approach enhances learning because it harnesses curiosity and is fueled by intrinsic motivation (Ortlieb, 2010).

Huizinga (1938) specifically addressed the motivating factor of word play, such as riddles and spelling contests, for achieving learning objectives in school settings. Like many other scholars of play, Huizinga (1938) acknowledged the power of play for enhancing retention of information (p. 34). Since then, many subsequent researchers and educators have expounded upon the power of play for teaching and learning. In fact, the American Academy of Pediatrics issued a clinical report that recommends a playful learning curriculum as a preferable method for teaching young learners (Yogman et al., 2018).

Play-Element in Gaming Culture

After several decades of relative obscurity, interest in the work of Huizinga was revived by computer game designers whose fascination with the magic circle concept inspired a closer look at *Homo Ludens.* Subsequent research projects and numerous publications by members of the gaming community increased the popularity of Huizinga as a resource for the study of play and games (Rodriguez, 2006; Salen & Zimmerman, 2003; Schell, 2020).

Play involves a rhythm of give and take, back and forth activity. In the parlance of Huizinga, this motion is noted in terms of the forces of *paidic* (game) and *ludic* (play) that interact in video games (Huizinga, 1938). Since all games will, in some degree, "reflect the moral and intellectual values of a culture, as well as contribute to their refinement and development" (Jones, 2008, p. 15), video games will reflect the social realities of the culture in which they are created. Thus, students of play will find that video games are worth studying not only as socio-cultural artifacts, but also for the ways that they demonstrate the centripetal and centrifugal dynamics of culture (Midgley, 2015).

Huizinga (1938) believed that the power of games to unify people and enable them to form a separate play community will continue after the game is over. The players, who are infused with a sense of togetherness, enjoy "the feeling of being 'apart together' in an exceptional situation, of sharing something important, of mutually withdrawing from the rest of the world and rejecting the usual norms" (p. 12). Furthermore, the "magic circle" mentioned by Huizinga is referred to as a "possibility space" among video game researchers, who observe that it facilitates more complex forms of play (Schell, 2020).

Schell (2020) examines the magic circle as a boundary to the game system when he states, "Much has been made of this boundary at the edge of the game. Johan Huizinga called it the magic circle and it does, indeed, have a magical feeling to it. When we are mentally 'in the game,' we have very different thoughts, feelings, and values than when we are 'out of the game.' How can games, which are nothing more than sets of rules, have this magical effect on us? To understand, we have to look to the human mind." (p.45) Ultimately, the designers of video games will continue to seek to push the limits of technology in order to encourage new, unrestricted forms of play, but the job of video game critics remains a simple one: to play (Salen & Zimmerman, 2003; Schell, 2020).

The viewpoints on play that Huizinga articulated, as well as his descriptions of the socio-cultural context that influence play and games, are relevant to the emerging field of game design as well as the analysis of video games. Digital media researchers compared the forces that changed pre-digital paidic games into ludic games with the addition of goal rules and ludic games into paidic games with metagaming. They explain how the possibility spaces in video games foster opportunities for even more play options. By examining the range of the paidia-ludis spectrum, researchers will continue to gain insights into the contextual framework of video gaming (Salen and Zimmerman, 2003).

CONCLUSION

In *Homo Ludens, A Study of the Play-Element in Culture*, Johan Huizinga endeavored to capture the elusive essence of play. He provided examples of the play-element from multiple perspectives and in a variety of contexts in the human experience. By doing so, he portrayed the role of the unconscious in human behavior and deepened the study of play. Huizinga declared that, although play is a topic that may seem unimportant to some, it is, in fact, an essential component of a fulfilling life. In his study of the play-element in humans, Huizinga emphasized that the development of culture is derived from a deep longing for the ludic experience. Huizinga would, most certainly, agree with scholars throughout the ages who affirm that ample time for play is critical for the healthy growth and development of children.

REFERENCES

Anchor, R. (1978). History and Play: Johan Huizinga and His Critics. *History and Theory, 17*, 1, 63–93. doi:10.2307/2504901.

Colie, R. (1964). Johan Huizinga and the Task of Cultural History. *The American Historical Review, 69*, 3, 607–630. doi:10.2307/1845780.

Edwards, J. (2013). Play and Democracy: Huizinga and the Limits of Agonism. *Political Theory, 41*,1, 90–115. Retrieved July 4, 2021, from http://www.jstor.org/stable/23484407.

Gadamer, H. (2004). *Truth and Method.* (J. Weinsheimer & D.G. Marshall, Trans.) Continuum.

Holst, J. (2017). The Dynamics of Play-Back to the Basics of Playing. *International Journal of Play, 6,* 1, 85–95. https://doi.org/10.1080/21594937.2017.1288383.

Huizinga, J. (1919). *The Autumn of the Middle Ages, Men and Ideas.* Edward Arnold Publishers.

Huizinga, J. (1924). *Erasmus and the Age of Reformation.* Charles Scribner's Sons.

Huizinga, J. (1938). *Homo Ludens: A Study of the Play-Element in Culture.* Random House.

Jones, S. E. (2008) *The Meaning of Video Games: Gaming and Textual Strategies*. New York: Routledge.

Midgley, A. (2015). Cultural History and the World of Johan Huizinga. *American Public University System: Saber and Scroll, 1,*1, 109–122.

Ortlieb, E. (2010). The Pursuit of Play within the Curriculum. *Journal of Instructional Psychology, 27,* 3, 241–246.

Peters, E. & Simons, W. (1999). The New Huizinga and the Old Middle Ages. *Speculum: A Journal of the Medieval Academy of America, 73,* 3, 587–620. doi/10.2307/2886762.

Rodriguez, H. (2006). The Playful and the Serious: An approximation to Huizinga's Homo Ludens. 6, 1. *Game Studies, The International Journal of Computer Game Research.* http://gamestudies.org/06010601/articles/rodriges.

Salen, K. & Zimmerman, E. (2003). *Rules of Play: Fundamentals of Game Design.* Massachusetts Institute of Technology.

Schell, J. (2020). *The Art of Game Design: A Book of Lenses, 3rd Edition.* Taylor & Francis.

Yogman, M., Garner, A., Hutchinson, J., Hirsh-Pasek, K., Michnick Golinkoff, R. (2018). The Power of Play: A Pediatric Role in Enhancing Development in Young Children. *Pediatrics, 1,* 142, 3.

5

Arnold Gesell

1880–1961

Marcy Guddemi

Arnold Gesell.

Play reveals the child's potential.

Arnold Lucius Gesell was an American clinical psychologist and medical doctor who is best known for his role in establishing the Gesell Institute, the Clinic of Child Development located in the Yale University Child Study Center. As a pioneer in the study of maturational development, Gesell is considered the father of child development (Salkind, 2004). Gesell acknowledged his role as the oldest of five siblings as well as his experience as a classroom teacher with his interest in human development (Miles, 1964).

GESELL'S OBSERVATIONS OF PLAY AND DEVELOPMENT

Throughout his body of work, Gesell expressed his belief in the value of play and its important role in child development. He stated that, from birth, children learn through play and that it never ceases to be "major business" because it is nature's way to meet the basic needs of development (Gesell & Ilg, 1946, p. 360). Like other theorists, he noted that

> play is his work, his business. When a child is playing, he concentrates with his whole being and acquires emotional satisfactions which he cannot get from other forms of activity. Deeply absorbing play seems to be essential for full mental growth. (Gesell & Ilg, 1946, pg. 360)

Arnold Gesell meticulously documented the chronological sequences, milestones, and behaviors in the development of normal children. He recorded personal-social, language, adaptive (cognitive), and motor growth from conception to the age of 10 years. Gesell was among the first researchers to enhance observation methods by filming children in action. By applying techniques that were novel at that time, including cinematography and a mesh dome lighted from inside that acted like a two-way mirror, he filmed and photographed children to document their development (Guddemi et al., 2014). Afterwards, he studied the films and utilize time-lapse photography in his efforts to discern patterns of behavior. Overall, Gesell applied his naturalistic survey approach to study the development of more than 10,000 children (Oliveira, 2018).

From these systematic observations, Gesell developed the maturational theory of child development. Findings from his study of the clinical films validated his beliefs in stages of development. As he stated in the book *The Child from Five to Ten,*

> The cycle of human development is continuous. All growth is based on previous growth. The growth process therefore is a paradoxical mixture of creation and

> of perpetuation. The child is always becoming something new; yet he always summates the essence of his past. (Gesell & Ilg, 1946, pg. 43)

During his years of study, Gesell observed that all children play and that a societal time period designated for childhood is directly related to the degree of maturity and complexity of the culture. He believed that play is nature's way to ensure that development is fulfilled to the fullest, so "developmental sequence, the patterns of play (will be) always conforming to the advancing patterns of maturity" (Gesell & Ilg, 1946, pg. 362).

Additionally, he observed that "play never ceases to be a major business throughout childhood. Nature plants strong play propensities in every normal child to make sure that certain basic needs of development will be satisfied" (Gesell & Ilg, 1946, pg. 360). Furthermore,

> Children reveal themselves most transparently in their play life. They play not from outer compulsion, but from inner necessity—the same kind of necessity which causes a kitten to chase a rolling ball . . . it involves a rehearsal of activities inherited from the ancestral generations. It is indeed a zestful merging of past, present and future. (Gesell & Ilg, 1946, pg. 359)

Influence on Parenting

Gesell and his colleagues published two books, *Infant and Child in the Culture of Today* (1943) and *The Child from Five to Ten* (1946), that were considered child development bibles for new parents. In a *New Yorker Magazine* article on Gesell, published in 1953, the accompanying cartoon illustrates a child reading Gesell's book saying to another boy his age, "Boy, what a stinker I am going to be next year!" (*New Yorker Magazine*, 1953).

Innate Capacity for Play

Gesell was influenced by Darwinism and he believed the human is what he is today because of evolution and the unique acculturation found in each family and society (Patrick, 1916). Because of this belief that all creatures evolved over time, he explained that the purpose of childhood play is to recapitulate the play of lesser species (Gesell & Ilg, 1940; Gesell & Ilg, 1943; Groos, 1898).

After years of observing children in person and in films, Gesell stated that nobody has to teach a child to play. He described a baby at play by saying,

> He flings his arms and flexes his legs (motor); he coos and chuckles (language), he fixates his eyes regardfully on fisted hand (adaptive), and he vocalizes on his

> mother's approach (personal-social). . . . He is ceaselessly . . . playing in one form or another. (Gesell & Ilg, 1946, pg. 359)

As children grow, they play peek-a-boo, clap hands, dump and drop, and chase, also with no apparent instruction. Gesell lamented the fact that adults often interfered with play.

> The culture directs, restrains and redirects these play impulses into approved channels, but always at the risk that the child will not get an optimal measure of the kind of play life which is best suited to his stage of maturity. All things considered, the modern child has too many set tasks and not a sufficient amount of untrammeled leisure and self-activity. (Gesell & Ilg, 1946, pg. 360)

Sequence of Play

Play may appear to be haphazard depending upon the availability of toys and playmates, but Gesell theorized that play is highly sequential, depending on the age and culture of the child, and is determined by developmental stages.

> Again and again, from child to child, do we find the same sequence repeated with increasing maturity: sand and water; doll and teddy bear; cars and wagons, tricycles and domestic doll play; dramatic play of story, hospital and school; reading; games, radio, bicycle, paper dolls; funny books. (Gesell & Ilg, 1946, pg. 360)

Because children usually remain true to their chronological age in the selection of spontaneous play choices, Gesell says, "This fact, itself, testifies to the basic significance of play in the dynamics of development" (Gesell & Ilg, 1946, p. 363).

Furthermore, Gesell stated that

> the role of play is many sided. Play is an outlet for obstructed and overflowing energy. It manifests exuberance in laughter, rollic (sic) and euphoria. Play is imitative, repetitive, or rhythmic in skipping, dancing, and dramatic expression. Play is psycho-motor exercise in running, jumping, tossing, hustling, balancing, and a host of gross and fine muscular activities. Play harks back to the past, in the emotional stirrings that accompany games of hunt, hide and seek, combat and chase, and in the quieter pastimes of exploring, collecting, hoarding, camping, and caring for flowers, plants and animals. Play penetrates the future, spurred by impulses of curiosity, experimentation, explosiveness and workmanship. In highly gifted children this workmanship declares itself in resourcefulness, originality or even in genius. (Gesell & Ilg, 1946, p. 362)

Like many researchers, Gesell theorized that play prepares children for later adult skills. He believed, as did his teacher G. Stanley Hall, that all creatures play and the time period designated for childhood is directly related to the degree of maturity and complexity of the culture (Hall, 1906). To explain his theory that the child develops within a process of acculturalization, he stated, "The child as an organism and the environment as a culture are separable. . . . The household is a cultural workshop for transmitting the social inheritance" (Gesell & Ilg, 1943).

Members of the early childhood profession who studied Gesell were intrigued by his work on the sequences of play along with Schedules and the Gradients of Child Development (Gesell, 1925). Thus, his theories contributed to the concept of developmentally appropriate practice, which is espoused by the National Association for the Education of Young Children (Copple & Bredekamp, 1987). Although today's sequences would include a plethora of technological toys, children still play with sand and water!

Constructivism in Play

Gesell's influential studies preceded the work of Piaget's, whose theory on child development became well known in America in the late 1960s and 1970s. Although their research was concurrent in the early to mid-1900s, and several letters of correspondence between the two exist (Ames, 1989), none indicate that they intentionally contributed to each other's work. In fact, Gesell's use of the word constructivism to explain play sequences is in contrast to the way that Piaget explains constructivism as the building of knowledge.

Interestingly, when Gesell described play, he noticed that the child first takes things out of the basket before he puts them back in. He observed that the child delights in demolishing a tower before he can build one and is more interested in taking a toy apart than putting it back together. He stated, "destructiveness, which may be a form of constructiveness in reverse . . . is a preparatory stage in the advancing maturity of play sequences" (Gesell & Ilg, 1946, p. 365).

Phantasy Play

Gesell mentions phantasy play in regard to fears and dreams. He noticed that, around the age of two, a child will begin to play imaginatively with objects; "Month by month his dramatic phantasy elaborates, because his nervous system is a growing structure" (Gesell &Ilg, 1946, p. 298). The sequence of this type of play goes from animating an object, to playing the role of the baby, playing with an imaginary object, impersonating an animal, impersonating another person, and perhaps having an alter ego type of imaginary companion. The imaginary playmate serves a purpose and leaves when the child no longer has use for it (Gesell & Ilg, 1946).

Pretend play was important to Gesell because he believed that it helps children prepare for future adult roles by acting out their fears and concerns. He elaborated on the topic of phantasy play when discussing play and pastimes. He explained that when a child becomes aggressive or violent during play, it may not be symbolic of inner urges or hostility, but rather practical and experimental. Gesell felt children primarily projected their "private mental images in a practical spirit, not a mean one. [The child] manipulates them in order to organize his concepts of reality" (Gesell & Ilg, 1946, p. 365).

Impact of Technology on Playtime

Arnold Gesell expressed concern for the ways that technology (TV, comics, radios, movies) and the overly organized preschool and primary school were replacing natural playtime. He was apprehensive about the long-term effects of technology on play and stated,

> They (technology) are a poor substitute for the more basic types of play which come from inner urges and which express the initiative and resourcefulness of the growing mind. Carried to excess . . . these recreational facilities lead to superficiality. (Gesell & Ilg, 1946, p. 396)

His fears were well justified. We now live in a society with children at risk because of the lack of play in early childhood settings and because the approved channels of appropriate behavior are so academically oriented (Almon and Miller, 2011).

CONCLUSION

If Gesell were alive today, he would probably be saddened by the prevalence of technology. From Mommy's cellphone in infancy to the proliferation of TVs, I-pads, video games, and school-age social media, technology is pervasive, which is possibly altering child development. Likewise, Gesell would also be concerned about the lack of free play in early education because

> the culture directs, restrains and redirects these play impulses into approved channels, but always at the risk that the child will not get an optimal measure of the kind of play life which is best suited to his stage of maturity. (Gesell & Ilg, 1946, p. 360)

According to the United Nations 1989 Convention on the Rights of the Child and its predecessor, the 1959 Declaration of Rights for Children, one of the fundamental rights of children is the right to play. Unquestionably, Gesell considered play not just a right, but rather a biological, intrinsic gift from nature to facilitate development. In fact, Gesell believed that play was predestined by nature to be a means to development and growth. The impressive legacy of Arnold Gesell is evidenced by the extensive archive of work that he created throughout his lifelong research, which continues to influence the study of child development and enriches our understanding of the value of play.

REFERENCES

Almon, J., & Miller, E. (2011). *The crisis in early education: A research-based case for more play and less pressure.* Alliance for Childhood.

Ames, L.B. (1989). *Arnold Gesell: Themes of his work.* Sciences Press, Inc.

Copple, C., & Bredekamp, S. (Eds.). (1987). *Developmentally appropriate practice in early childhood programs serving children from birth through age 8*. National Association for the Education of Young Children.

Gesell, A. (1925). *The mental growth of the pre-school child: A psychological outline of normal development from birth to the sixth year, including a system of developmental diagnosis*. Macmillan.

Gesell, A., & Ilg, F. (1940). *The first five years of life*. Harper.

Gesell, A., & Ilg, F. (1943). *Infant and child in the culture of today*. Harper.

Gesell, A., & Ilg, F. (1946). *The child from five to ten*. Harper.

Groos, K. (1898). *The play of animals.* Appleton.

Guddemi, M., Sambrook, A., Randel, B., Fite, K., Selva, G., Gagnon, K. (2014). Arnold Gesell's developmental assessment revalidation substantiates child-oriented curriculum. SAGE Open Volume 4, Number 2.

Guddemi, M., & Selva, G. (2014). *Pretend play and brain growth: The link to learning and academic success.* Gesell Institute of Child Development.

Hall, G. S. (1906). *Youth: Its education, regiment, and hygiene.* Appleton.

Miles, W. (1964). *Arnold Lucius Gesell (1880–1961): A biographical memoir.* National Academy of Sciences.

New Yorker Magazine, Cartoon, March 21, 1953 Issue. Page 37.

Oliveira, P. (2018). Our proud heritage. True then, truer now: The enduring contributions of Arnold Gesell. *Young Children, 73, 3*, 87–89.

Patrick, G. T. W. (1916). *The psychology of relaxation.* Houghton Mifflin.

Salkind, N. (2004). *An introduction to theories of human development.* Sage Publications. DOI: http://dx.doi.org/10.4135/9781483328676.

Yale Child Study Center (2021). "Our history>Child Study Center-Yale School of Medicine. Retrieved from https://medicine.yale.edu/childstudy/.

6

Margaret Naumburg

1890–1983

Blythe Hinitz, Jeroen Staring, and Jerry Aldridge

Margaret Naumburg.

Children express their inner lives through play.

Margaret Naumburg was a pioneer in the field of art therapy and is well known for her commitment to free expression. Perhaps more than any other progressive educator of the early twentieth century, Naumburg focused on individual free play (Hinitz, 2013). She believed that it was only through the individual child's own direction, as expressed through free play, that she or he could express unconscious conflicts and bring them into the light of consciousness to work through them. In other words, individual free play taps into a child's inner world (Naumburg, 1947).

BIOGRAPHICAL SKETCH

Naumburg grew up in Manhattan, attended Vassar and Barnard, and later studied with John Dewey at Columbia University. In 1913, she received a Montessori diploma after completing the First International Montessori Teacher Training Course with Maria Montessori in Italy (Hinitz, 2013). Later,

> Naumburg returned to New York City to open her first class, with musician Claire Raphael. . . . After one year of teaching, Naumburg felt that the formal Montessori Method was too restricting, and she modified the curriculum when she and Raphael moved their class to 60th Street in 1914. (Hinitz, 2013, p. 182)

Naumburg's return to New York marked the beginning of the first Montessori School in the United States (Altman, 2009), which later became the Children's School (Staring, Bouchard, & Aldridge, 2014). Then, in 1922, Naumburg renamed her school Walden School. After leaving Walden School, Margaret Naumburg pursued her interest in art therapy, schizophrenic and psychoneurotic art (Naumburg, 1950, 1953), and dynamically oriented art therapy (1966).

Psychoanalytic and Analytical Psychology Underpinnings

While Margaret Naumburg was a leader in the progressive school movement, she developed her own unique ideas about the importance and purpose of play. A salient example was her understanding and implementation of play from the viewpoint of Jungian analytical psychology. Specifically, "Naumburg herself underwent three years of analysis with Jungian psychiatrist Beatrice Hinkle and later she did further analysis with Freudian A. A. Brill (a Walden school parent)" (Hinitz, 2013, p. 181; consult Naumburg, 1917, 1919). She also encouraged the teachers and staff members to undertake analysis for themselves (Staring, Aldridge, & Christensen, 2018). But how did this translate into children's free play in the classroom?

First, Naumburg advocated for a need for change from traditional views of education and play to a psychoanalytic perspective. She wrote:

> Up to the present, our methods of education have dealt only with the conscious or surface mental life of the child. The new analytic psychology has, however, demonstrated that the unconscious mental life, which is the outgrowth of the child's instincts, plays a greater role than the conscious. . . . This discovery of the fundamental sources of thought and action must bring about a readjustment in education. School problems can no longer be dealt with as they appear on the surface, for our deeper knowledge we must direct our attention to the deeper realities beneath. (Naumburg, 1917, p. 7; 1919, p. 242)

Based on analytical psychology and psychoanalysis, the inner world of children was a prominent focus of free play. While many progressive schools in the early 1900s emphasized the social and cooperative nature of play through jointly exploring the "here and now" of the school and neighborhood (Mitchell, 1921), Naumburg (1922, 1928) encouraged more "free play" initiated and carried out by the individual child. The idea of "free expression" without directive was promoted, while adults observed, recorded, and attempted to understand a child's inner world from her or his play (Naumburg, 1947). Furthermore, a child's inner world of experience, including fantasy and fiction, was not discouraged, as it was in other progressive schools, such as Lucy Sprague Mitchell's School for Children at the Bureau of Educational Experiments where "reality" or non-fiction play was encouraged (Aldridge & Horns-Marsh, 1991; Mitchell, 1921; Staring, Aldridge, & Christensen, 2018).

In a letter to artist Gladys Brown Ficke, Naumburg later explained,

> Of course, the study of the child by means of the psychoanalytic approach is of primary importance, and I have emphasized this in my educational work for forty years . . . many of the analysts do not realize that as early as 1914 I took my stand on the importance of psychoanalysis in relation to education. As far as I know, I was the first person in the U.S. to apply it to education in the development of the Walden School. But at that time, it was like a voice crying in the wilderness. (Naumburg, 1954)

Art as Play

Although Naumburg did not explicitly talk about art as play, her conception of art therapy was analogous to her notions of child play. For example, Naumburg did not believe in the extensive use of patterns, coloring sheets, or predetermined art projects, just as she did not believe in imposed structures on a child's play. She continued this practice in art therapy decades after she left Walden School.

Naumburg (1947) stated,

> As soon as original art work is encouraged, instead of dependence on models and specific techniques, the focus of a patient's art activity is modified. He will begin to draw on his own inner resources and this will inevitably lead to some expression of the conflicts within the personality, which may reveal aspects of the patterns of his mental disease as well as the specific insecurities or traumatic experiences within the patient. (p. 50)

Just as the inner world of a child is represented through play, so too, a child reveals her or his true nature through open-ended art (Wickes, 1927).

An Amalgam of Dance, Music and Awareness Methods

In 1915, in their Montessori classes, Naumburg and Raphael offered an amalgam of dance, music, and awareness methods in order to instigate "free expression" and "free play." In a May 1915 newspaper article, Naumburg gave details regarding her Montessori classes' curriculum:

> We have accepted Dr. Montessori's work with keen appreciation of its great value . . . and we have added to it what we have learned from other great teachers, from Froebel and Dalcroze, and Miss Bentley, and most recently from Mr. Matthias Alexander, of London. (Naumburg in Rodman, 1915; see also Hinitz, 2002, p. 43)

Earlier, Naumburg (1913) had already published about Montessori. She also issued an article regarding her newly won views about Dalcroze Eurhythmics (Naumburg, 1914b). Claire Raphael, who in 1913 had studied T. H. Yorke Trotter's Rhythmic Method of teaching music classes in London, had motivated Naumburg to study Eurhythmics as well as dance educator, Alys E. Bentley's Interpretive Dancing (Hinitz, 2013; Staring, Bouchard, & Aldridge, 2014).

The last, but rather unknown ingredient in Naumburg and Raphael's amalgam of dance, music, and awareness methods to instigate "free expression" and "free play" consisted of what later became known as the Alexander Technique.

The Alexander Technique

Ten years after Tasmanian *vaudeville* stage artist, and elocution, voice and breathing teacher Frederick Matthias Alexander emigrated to London in

1904, he began working in New York City, where he taught his methods of improving motor coordination and breathing habits between 1914 and 1924 (Staring, 2005). Alexander evolved into a teacher in re-education of habits of posture, moving the body, and breathing. Later, he would be known as the founder of the Alexander Technique (Bloch, 2004).

While Alexander lived in Manhattan, diverse Columbia University scholars took lessons (e.g., John Dewey and Wesley C. Mitchell). They were very satisfied with the results. When Alexander published his book, *Man's Supreme Inheritance* in 1918, several leading academics wrote book reviews full of praise. While Dora Thompson (1919) of the New York City Washington Irving High School estimated that Alexander had "a message of supreme importance to the American public, especially in this time of educational reorganization" (p. 23), John Dewey (1918) stated,

> all interested in educational reform may well remember freedom of physical action and free expression of emotion are means, not ends, and that as means they are justified only in so far as they are used as conditions for developing power of intelligence. The substitution of control by intelligence for control by external authority, not the negative principle of no control or the spasdomic [*sic.*] principle of control by emotional gusts, is the only basis upon which reformed education can build. (Dewey, 1918, pp. xvi–xvii)

At the time, New York harbored several institutions that strove for radical educational renewal—for instance, the Bureau of Educational Experiments (BEE), chaired by Lucy Sprague Mitchell. The majority of its members were experienced educational reformers who had previously worked for the Public Education Association of the City of New York, the Gary School League, and the Fairhope League.

The Bureau of Educational Experiments collected and shared information about progressive education initiatives, conducted and reported educational experiments, and subsidized a number of schools. Among these was the Play School (later renamed City and Country School)—founded in 1913 by Caroline Pratt, a BEE charter member. In addition, the BEE published bulletins on experimental schools like Pratt's Play School and Naumburg's the Children's School. What is important in this context of educational experiments and renewal is the fact that both Naumburg and Raphael shared educational visions with BEE members. Both spoke in favor of radical education reform and both were members of the Gary School League.

Naumburg's Influence on Progressive Thought and Schools related to Free Play

Elizabeth Irwin, Marietta Johnson, Harriet M. Johnson, Lucy Sprague Mitchell, Margaret Naumburg, Caroline Pratt, Claire Raphael (Reis) and John Dewey mutually influenced each other through their interactions over the years in progressive education and political circles. Margaret Naumburg, her various Montessori classes, the Children's School, and Walden School had a profound influence on progressive thought and education during the 1900s.

> Walden served as one of the original sites for the Bureau of Education Experiments (BEE) student teachers. When the BEE was founded by Lucy Sprague Mitchell, Caroline Pratt, and Harriet Johnson in 1916, there were very few schools to which they could send students for practicum experiences. (Hinitz, 2013, p. 205)

As a result, Walden School received many students from the BEE, including Harriet K. Cuffaro and Polly Greenburg. "It continued to serve as an influential educational laboratory into the 1980s, welcoming students and instructors from Teachers College of Columbia University, Bank Street College, New York University, Queens College and other teacher education institutions in and around New York City" (Hinitz, 2013, p. 205). No doubt, the student teachers were immersed in the Walden philosophy of individual free play based on analytical psychology and psychoanalysis, as well as on dance, music, and awareness methods.

The Contrasting Contexts of Naumburg's Educational Ideas about Free Play

Maria Montessori. As noted earlier, in 1913 Naumburg was part of the very first group of outsiders to receive teaching training in the Montessori Method under Maria Montessori in Rome. Naumburg wanted to be a pioneer in this new method. She developed a personal relationship with Montessori early in the course, but this did not last. "Naumburg's enthusiasm for the Montessori method waned and a personality conflict arose between these two intellectual, strong-willed women" (Naumburg, n.d., p. 3; Lascarides & Hinitz, 2011, p. 303). Decades later, in a letter to Sol Cohen, Naumburg explained,

> I saw a good deal of her personally in the first part of the course. Later in the term when she took me for a drive with her she asked me why I had withdrawn from her and I told her the truth. That I found her authoritarian in imposing her

> ideas and was not concerned with accepting everything she said without question. (Naumburg, 1967, p. 3)

After returning to the United States and experiencing Jungian analysis under Beatrice Hinkle during the years 1914–1917, Naumburg's notions of play moved even further away from Montessori's. Naumburg did not believe materials should be used in only one way and the strict guidelines of Montessori regarding play were abandoned.

John Dewey. Naumburg developed a close, personal relationship with John Dewey and his family. Even before introducing Dewey to F. Matthias Alexander and his methods, there were numerous other connections with the Deweys. "Margaret studied with John Dewey during her undergraduate and graduate course work at Columbia University. He became a professional mentor and friend" (Hinitz, 2013, p. 184). Over time, her ideas diverged from Dewey's, particularly with regard to the focus on the individual versus the group and to play. Naumburg encouraged individual free play that focused on the inner world of childhood. She believed that the problem in the United States was "too great an emphasis on group life" (Hinitz, 2013, p. 186). She encouraged the need to "develop an individualism that is socially responsive" (Naumburg, 1930, p. 6).

Dewey focused more on social realities, as he expounded in an article in *The New Republic*. He explained,

> [N]o one can justly decry the value of any education which supplies additions to the resources of the inner life of pupils. But surely the problem of progressive education demands that this result be not effected in such a way as to ignore or obscure preparation for the social realities—including the evils—of industrial and political civilization. (Dewey, 1930, p. 206)

Marietta Johnson. Naumburg enrolled in the Organic Education teacher training course under Johnson at the Fairhope Summer School in Greenwich, Connecticut (Naumburg, 1914a). While Johnson provided some structured physical activity, such as dance, in the Fairhope School of Organic Education, she also emphasized the individual child's need for free play and respected a child's choices with regard to the child's materials and expression in play. In her school,

> It was Marietta Johnson's wish that children would maintain a sense of wonder throughout their adult lives. Children didn't receive report cards or grades, did not have homework, and were not allowed to fail at the Organic School. They learned within a context that supported and nurtured their own ideas and interests. (Aldridge & Christensen, 2013, p. 67)

Parting Thoughts

What can educators conclude about Margaret Naumburg's beliefs and practices concerning free play? A cursory glance at Naumburg's life and works could result in the notion that she was eclectic in her approach to play. After all, Naumburg studied with disparate groups of pundits of education, including Maria Montessori, John Dewey, Marietta Johnson, and F. Matthias Alexander. She was analyzed by Jungian psychoanalyst Beatrice Hinkle and later by Freudian psychiatrist, Abraham A. Brill (Hutchins, 2018). However, her beliefs about free play were probably most similar to those of Beatrice Hinkle, and her practices administered at her consecutive Montessori classes, the Children's School, and Walden School were not that different from those experienced at Marietta Johnson's Organic School.

Thus, five conclusions can be drawn about Naumburg and free play: 1) her focus on individual free play; 2) her belief in the inner world of the child; 3) her emphasis on choice in free play; 4) her promotion of active learning (both mental and physical); and, lastly, 5) her use of free play as problem solving.

Individual free play. Perhaps more than any other progressive educator of the early twentieth century, Naumburg focused on individual free play. It was only through the individual child's own direction, expressed through free play that she or he was able to express unconscious conflicts and tensions and bring them into the light of consciousness and work through them. In other words, individual free play taps into a child's inner world (Naumburg, 1947).

Inner world of the child. According to Naumburg, free play was the child's vehicle for dealing with inner conflict through outer actions. Just as the inner world of a child is represented through play, so too, a child reveals her or his true nature through open-ended art (Naumburg, 1921).

Choice in free play. Unlike many progressive educators, Naumburg believed almost exclusively in individual choice in free play. In Naumburg's judgment, the child should choose the form and function free play takes, which is most often based on the child's unconscious needs (Naumburg, 1921).

Active learning in free play. Naumburg also believed that free play involved active learning, both mental and physical. Free play could take any form if chosen by the child, including free expression through art, dance, music, and other forms of mental and/or physical activity (Naumburg, 1921).

Free play as problem solving. A child was capable of solving her or his own problems through free play, according to Naumburg. A child who is always directed will not learn how to experiment, create, or invent new ways to experience those materials (Naumburg, 1921).

CONCLUSION

In the twenty-first century, it may be time to reconsider Naumburg's beliefs and practices concerning free play, especially in an ever increasing age of a push down curriculum, in which all decisions are made for the child before she or he enters the classroom—unfortunately, even regarding how and when to play, if the child is ever allowed to do so.

REFERENCES

Aldridge, J., & Christensen, L. M. (2013). *Stealing from the mother: The marginalization of women in education and psychology from 1900–2010.* Rowman & Littlefield.

Aldridge, J., & Horns-Marsh, V. (1991). Contributions and applications of analytical psychology to education and child development. *Journal of Instructional Psychology, 18*, 3, 151–158.

Altman, J. (2009). Margaret Naumburg. Online available: http://jwa.org/encyclopedia/article/naumburg-margaret

Bloch, M. (2004). *F. M.: The life of F. Matthias Alexander, founder of the Alexander Technique.* Little Brown.

Dewey, J. (1918). Introductory word. In F. M. Alexander, *Man's supreme inheritance: Conscious guidance and control in relation to human evolution in civilization* (pp. xii–xvii). E. P. Dutton & Company.

Dewey, J. (1930, July 9). How much freedom in the new schools? *The New Republic*, 204–206.

Hinitz, B. F. (2002). Margaret Naumburg and the Walden School. In A. R. Sadnovnik, & S. F. Semel (eds.), *Founding mothers and others. Women educational leaders during the progressive era* (pp. 37–59). Palgrave.

Hinitz, B. F. (2013). The impact of Margaret Naumburg and Walden School on early childhood education in the United States. In B. F. Hinitz (ed.), *The hidden history of early childhood education* (pp. 181–212). Routledge.

Hutchins, A. A. (2018, January 31). Margaret Naumburg Papers; Ms. Coll. 294 (Update January 31, 2018). Philadelphia, PA: University of Pennsylvania, Kislak Center for Special Collections, Rare Books and Manuscripts.

Lascarides, V. C., & Hinitz, B. F. (2011) *History of early childhood education.* Routledge.

Mitchell, L. S. (1921). *Here and now story book.* E. P. Dutton & Company.

Naumburg, M. (1913, December 13). Maria Montessori: Friend of children. *The Outlook,* 796–799.

Naumburg, M. (1914a). *Montessori class: The house of children.* New York: privately printed. Margaret Naumburg Papers, Annenburg Rare Book & Manuscript Library. Van Pelt Dietrich Library Center, University of Pennsylvania.

Naumburg, M. (1914b, January 17). The Dalcroze idea: What Eurhythmics is and what it means. *The Outlook,* 127–131.

Naumburg, M. (1917). A direct method of education. In M. Naumburg & C. L. Deming (eds.), *Experimental schools: Bulletin number four* (7–11). Bureau of Educational Experiments.

Naumburg, M. (1919, September). A direct method of education. *The Modern School,* 242–247.

Naumburg, M. (1921). *The children's school.* New York: privately printed.

Naumburg, M. (1922). Life in a new school. *The World Tomorrow,* *5*(9), 265–266.

Naumburg, M. (1928). *The child and the world: Dialogues in modern education.* Harcourt, Brace, and Company.

Naumburg, M. (1930, April 26). Personal correspondence with John Dewey. Margaret Naumburg Papers, Annenberg Rare Book & Manuscript Library, Van Pelt Dietrich Library Center, University of Pennsylvania.

Naumburg, M. (1947). *Studies of the "free" expression of behavior problem children as a means of diagnosis and therapy.* Coolidge Foundation.

Naumburg, M. (1950). *Schizophrenic art: Its meaning in psychotherapy.* Grune & Stratton, Inc.

Naumburg, M. (1953). *Psychoneurotic art: Its function in psychotherapy.* Grune & Stratton, Inc.

Naumburg, M. (1954). Letter to Gladys Ficke, July 7, 1954. Jeroen Staring Collection.

Naumburg, M. (1966). *Dynamically oriented art therapy: Its principles and practice.* Grune & Stratton, Inc.

Naumburg, M. (1967). Letter to Sol Cohen, January 25, 1967, Folder 147, in Margaret Naumburg papers, Ms. Coll. 294. Philadelphia: University of Pennsylvania Finding Aids, Penn Libraries.

Naumburg, M. (n.d.). Margaret Naumburg papers, Ms. Coll. 294. Philadelphia: University of Pennsylvania Finding Aids, Penn Libraries.

Rodman, H. (1915, May 5). East Side pupils think in rhythm. *The New York Tribune,* 5.

Staring, J. (2005). *Frederick Matthias Alexander 1869–1955: The origins and history of the Alexander Technique.* Nijmegen, The Netherlands: Integraal.

Staring, J., Aldridge, J., & Christensen, L. M. (2018). The influence of Beatrice Hinkle and Jungian psychology on the early progressive school movement in the United States. *International Journal of Case Studies,* *7*(11), 35–43.

Staring, J., Bouchard, E., & Aldridge, J. (2014). New light on the early history of Walden School. *International Journal of Case Studies,* *3*(9), 1–21.

Wilkes, F. G. (1927). *The inner world of childhood: A study in analytical psychology.* New York: Appleton.

7

Jean Piaget

1896–1980

Olga S. Jarrett

Jean Piaget.

Play is the work of the child.

What is play, how does it differ by stage, and how does it promote development? According to Piaget, "if every act of intelligence is an equilibrium between assimilation and accommodation, while imitation is a continuation of accommodation for its own sake, it may be said conversely that play is essentially assimilation, or the primacy of assimilation over accommodation" (Piaget, 1945/1962, p. 87). Piaget's research on play was initially conducted with his own three children who early began to imitate him with pleasure and engage in behaviors without an obvious purpose such as sucking without drinking. Seemingly, repeating behaviors without purpose except to make interesting things happen was, for Piaget, early play.

RESEARCHER AND THEORIST

Jean Piaget had a very broad background based on his many interests (*Britannica*, 2017). His initial pursuit was biology, leading to his first publication at age 11 on a part-albino sparrow he found, continuing with publications and work at a museum on classification of mollusks during his teenage years, and culminating in a PhD in the natural sciences with a dissertation on mollusks. However, his godfather introduced him to philosophy, which, combined with the natural sciences, promoted his interest in genetic epistemology, the study of the origins of knowledge. He explored psychoanalytic theory with Carl Jung for a semester in Zurich followed by two years studying abnormal psychology and intelligence with Theodore Simon, a founder of intelligence testing, at the Alfred Binet Laboratory in Paris (Voyat, 1980).

In administering IQ tests for standardization, Piaget became more interested in children's incorrect answers and their reasoning at various ages, leading to his lifelong interest in how children acquire knowledge. Piaget's research included data collection in a Montessori-inspired school, playing marbles with children of various ages, detailed observations of his own three children during infancy, and clinical interviews with larger numbers of children with staff at his International Centre for Genetic Epistemology in Geneva. His research and publications included how language and thought develops (Piaget, 1923/2009), the child's conception of number (Piaget, 1941/1965) physical causality (Piaget, 1930/1972), the child's construction of reality (Piaget, 1937/1954), the child's conception of the nature of the world (Piaget, 1926/1951), and two books especially relevant to the importance of play in his theory of development, *Play, Dreams, and Imitation in Childhood* (Piaget, 1945/1962) and *The Moral Judgment of the Child* (Piaget,

1932/1997). Piaget never considered his theory completed, always thinking of himself as "the chief revisionist of Piaget" (Piaget, 1970, p. 703).

Nature and Role of Play

According to Piaget, his own children exhibited early play behaviors by imitation (accommodation) and repeated them for pleasure, assimilating them into their repertoire of behaviors. Our two-year-old grandson intently watched an elephant at the zoo and was intrigued with its trunk. Several months later, while we were resting during a walk at a public garden, he *became* an elephant, crouching down, creating a trunk with one arm, and calling out, "I'm an elephant. Look, I'm an elephant." He insisted we not move from that spot for about 30 minutes while he continued to be an elephant, moving from imitation to play, assimilating "elephant-ness."

Games Children Play

According to Piaget, there are "three main types of structure which characterize children's *games* [probably better translated as *play*] and determine their classification. There are practice games, symbolic games, and games with rules, while constructional games constitute the transition from all three to adapted behaviors" (Piaget, 1945/1962, p. 110). The sensorimotor child engages in practice play, whereas symbolic play predominates during the preoperational stage, and games with rules become salient during concrete operations.

Across these stages, the child contructs, at various levels of complexity. In this sequence, a baby might bat at spoons hanging above her crib, a two-year-old might use a spoon to feed a teddy bear, and an eight-year-old might construct a board game using a spoon as a pusher. Or, the sensorimotor child might chew, bang, or stack two blocks, the preoperational child might make a tall stack of blocks or turn the blocks into a zoo, while the concrete or formal operational child might hammer or screw the blocks together to make bookends or a sculpture (Piaget, 1945/1962).

In a study of the game of marbles, Piaget interviewed children of various ages on how they played marbles, correlating their understanding of the rules with their moral understandings (Piaget, 1932/1997). Introducing himself as someone who had forgotten how to play marbles, he asked boys (apparently Swiss girls do not play marbles) from 2-13 how to play marbles, a game that children often learn from other, older children. From their answers and demonstrations, he developed a sequence of stages in marble playing, from tossing the marbles about with no rules, through thinking the rules of marbles are immutable (established by one's father or even by God), to a formal operations assumption that rules vary in different locales and can be changed by agreement (Piaget, 1932/1997).

Piaget's conclusions fit his theory on how thinking about rules and fairness changes across the stages, conclusions corroborated by his interviews with children regarding moral conflict stories (Piaget, 1932/1997). But by studying a game with rules, his research also raises the question of what children learn about justice, honesty, and fairness through playing various games with rules with same-age classmates. Do children go through the same stages when they play only adult determined games, as in team sports or instructional games led by the teacher? Do they learn the same things about fairness? Do they learn as much about fairness from structured programs during recess as they do from free play?

Piaget's Relationships with Other Thinkers on Play

Piaget commented on his contemporaries who have also influenced thinking and application on children's play, including Maria Montessori, Lev Vygotsky, and Brian Sutton-Smith. Piaget conducted some of his early research at a "modified Montessori institution," was president of the Swiss Montessori Society, and agreed with Montessori on many things. They were both constructivists, believing that children construct their own understandings using what would be considered play materials (Piaget- Montessori Answers, n.d.). They differed in the age at which children should be exposed to formal learning, with Piaget preferring to wait until the stage of concrete operations at around seven.

Montessori believed there were "sensitive periods" of development and that many children were ready to learn various concepts at an earlier age. Piaget and Montessori also differed in how much children's play materials should be structured. Montessori created orderly environments where the children's materials were designed to most efficiently teach certain concepts. In contrast, Piaget was less concerned about teaching than enabling children to figure out concepts on their own by playing with objects and materials in their environment. Montessori referred to the active materials she designed for children as their work. However, this work includes many aspects of play—active, enjoyable, and to some extent, freely chosen (DeVries with Kohlberg, 1987).

Piaget and Vygotsky commented on one another's theories of development. In a preface written for the Russian translation of Piaget's early books, Vygotsky expressed admiration for Piaget but was critical of Piaget's focus on egocentric talk, believing egocentrism depends not only on age but also on how social the child's world is. According to Vygotsky,

> Piaget observed children at play together in a particular kindergarten, and his coefficients are valid only for this special child milieu. When the children's activity consists entirely of play, it is accompanied by extensive soliloquizing. Stern points out that in a German kindergarten, in which there was more group activity, the coefficient of egocentrism was somewhat lower, and that in the home children's speech tends to be predominantly social at a very early age. If that is true of German children, the difference between Soviet children and Piaget's children in the Geneva kindergarten must be even greater. (Vygotsky, 1932, p. 17)

Sadly, Vygotsky's work was not available in French until much later and Piaget's response, in which he agreed with much of Vygotsky's criticism, was written after Vygotsky's early death. Piaget concluded that "all logical thought is socialized because it implies the possibility of communication between individuals (Piaget, 1962/2000, p. 254). He did not disagree with Vygotsky's views on play.

Finally, Piaget and the eminent play theorist, Brian Sutton-Smith, exchanged views on play in *Psychological Review* in 1966 (republished in *Child's Play* by Herron and Sutton-Smith, 1971a). Their discussion begins with Sutton-Smith's critique of Piaget conclusions in *Play, Dreams and Imitation in Childhood*, followed by Piaget's response, and concluding with Sutton-Smith's reply. Sutton-Smith (1971) admires Piaget's meticulous study of early play as (with the possible exception of psychoanalytic theory) "the most conceptually elaborate account of play yet to be presented and, in addition, includes the best available examples of the sequence of play activities in the first years of life" (p. 326). However, he is critical that Piaget housed his theory of play within his theory of intelligence.

Sutton-Smith claims linking play with intelligence is better at explaining intelligence that humans and mollusks have in common than explaining the connections between play and art and creativity. He calls Piaget's theory a "copy theory" in which play is reduced to a copy of what is accommodated (Sutton-Smith, 1971a). Piaget (1971, p. 337) responded, "I must confess that I have some difficulty in recognizing the opinions that this author attributes to me, and I think that his formulations of them derive from the fact that he has only been able to assess that portion of my work that has been translated into English." Piaget insisted that for him, knowledge is not a copy of reality, but "to know or to understand is to transform reality" and play becomes more adapted to reality with age as children engage in less fantasy play and more construction play (1971, p. 337).

Sutton-Smith's rejoinder was that play serves not only a tension reducing cognitive function, but also is a means of self-expression exhibited in festivals and challenges like mountaineering and tight-rope walking that are tension enhancing. Therefore, he asserts that some forms of play are not explained by Piaget's theory (Sutton-Smith, 1971b).

The Purpose of Education According to Piaget

In his books on education, *To Understand Is to Invent: The Future of Education* (1918/1977) and *Science of Education and the Psychology of the Child* (1935/1969), Piaget shares insights on the importance, purpose, and methods of education. In an era when test scores determine whether schools are considered failing, whether teachers get raises, whether schools are closed or assigned a "turn-around officer," and whether real estate values go up or down (depending on Zillow Real Estate ratings of schools), Piaget's goals for education may sound unusual:

> The principal goal of education is to create men [women too] who are capable of doing new things, not simply of repeating what other generations have done—men [women] who are creative, inventive, and discoverers. The second goal of education is to form minds which can be critical, can verify, and not accept everything they are offered. The great danger today is of slogans, collective opinions, ready-made trends of thoughts. We have to be able to resist individually, to criticize, to distinguish between what is proven and what is not. So, we need pupils who are active, who learn early to find out by themselves, partly by their own spontaneous activity and partly through material we set up for them; who learn early to tell what is verifiable and what is simply the first idea to come to them. (Piaget, 1973, p. 35)

Applications to Contemporary Educational Practices

So, what does this have to do with play? In his books on education, Piaget discussed the need for more specialized training in math and science, more active methods for children four to six, application of child and adolescent psychology in teaching, and focus on the interdisciplinary rather than compartmentalized nature of knowledge (Piaget, 1918/1977). What do active methods in the classroom look like? According to Piaget,

> the basic principle of active methods will have to draw its inspiration from the history of science and may be expressed as follows: to understand is to discover, or reconstruct by rediscovery, and such conditions must be complied with if in the future individuals are to be formed who are capable of production and creativity and not simply repetition. (Piaget, 1918/1977, p. 20)

In other words, students should learn science basically the way Piaget studied his children (and eventually many other children), systematically by making careful observations. A fascinating article compares Piaget and Michael Faraday, the natural scientist who experimented with electromagnetism and electromagnetic induction, in the way they played with ideas and developed experiments (Cavicchi, 2006).

Piaget was definitive on the need for active methods of teaching children of all ages (Piaget, 1935/1969) and considered the play element of activity especially important for young children. He bemoaned the fact that play is "neglected by the traditional school because it appears to them to be devoid of functional significance" (p. 155). For Piaget, play was not just relaxation (recess) but was an important aspect of adaptation, the essence of intelligence. Piaget (1935/1969) asserted,

> The complete adaptation that it is childhood's task to achieve consists in a progressive synthesis of assimilation and accommodation. This is why, in the course of its own internal development, the play of small children is gradually transformed into adapted constructions requiring an ever-increasing amount of what is in effect work, to such an extent that in the infant classes [primary classes] of an active school every kind of spontaneous transition may be observed between play and work. (p. 157)

Piaget did not develop programs for young children based on his theory. That work has been carried out by interpreters of his theory, including Piaget's mentees and their mentees who implemented Piaget's ideas in America. Constance Kamii, Seymour Papert, and Eleanor Duckworth worked directly with Piaget. Other scholars, including Rheta DeVries, Betty Zan, Mitchel Resnick, George E. Foreman, and Lawrence Kohlberg, extended Piaget's theories and developed and/or researched constructivist programs. Play and playfulness has been a very important part of all these programs.

Kamii and DeVries, inspired by Piaget's research with the game of marbles, wrote books both on physical knowledge and group games from Piaget's perspective. Their book on group games (Kamii & DeVries, 1980), with a forward by Piaget, describes children's games with ways teachers can adapt them so children can learn more about physical and moral aspects of their play. Kamii has since focused on applying Piaget to the learning of math while DeVries along with Betty Zan focused on teaching physics to young children through ramps, pathways, blocks, and marbles (DeVries and Sales, 2011; Counsell, Escalada, Geiken, Sander, Uhlenberg, Van Meeteren, Yoshizawa, & Zan, 2016).

Kohlberg's books (Kohlberg, 1987; DeVries & Kohlberg, 1987), show Piaget's influence in the area of moral development. From Piaget's two stages of moral understanding (Piaget, 1932/1997) developed from the game of marbles, Kohlberg identified eight stages of moral development, from concrete operations through formal operations.

Piaget also influenced science education. Eleanor Duckworth, graduate student and Research and Teaching Assistant with Piaget and Inhelder in Geneva (Duckworth, n.d.) worked with the Elementary Science Study (ESS) to make science more hands-on and understandable. In *The Having of Wonderful Ideas* (2006), she considers ideas "the essence of intellectual development," based on Piaget's ideas on intelligence, play, and creativity.

Seymour Papert, who worked with Piaget at the University of Geneva, adapted Piaget's ideas of constructivism to a theory he called "constructionism" (Blikstein, n.d.). As an MIT faculty member, he applied constructionism to children's manipulations with a computer program he called "Logo," allowing children to move a robotic "turtle" around the room. Papert predicted the importance of the computer in education (Papert, 1982/1993) and the name of his book, *Mindstorms* gave its name to LEGO robotics. Papert worked with LEGO to develop fun, challenging ways for children to build and program toys. His attempt to influence schools to use computers creatively (Papert, 1993) was only partially successful, but his former doctoral student, Mitchel Resnick, Professor of Learning Research in the Lifelong Kindergarten Research Group at the MIT Media Lab, has continued his work.

According to Resnick (2017, p. 7), "kindergarten learning is exactly what's needed to help people of all ages develop the creative capacities needed to thrive in today's rapidly changing society." Resnick influenced a movement where children are free to tinker, explore, and build their own understandings of the world. Marina Bers, student of Papert and Resnick has applied Piaget's ideas to her work of infusing technology in the early childhood classroom (Bers, 2008).

Final Thoughts

As a researcher, Piaget was meticulous in his methods. Psychologists and philosophers in general and genetic epistemologists in particular developed theories that made sense from their thinking and experience. In contrast, Piaget drew his conclusions from data he collected systematically. When asked, in his last interview, about his "system," he responded: "I would first like to say when you talk of my system that I have no system. I have never constructed a system in the abstract so as to try later to verify it factually. What is called the system are the serial interpretations that I have given to new facts that we have discovered in my research" (Voyat, 1980, no page numbers). It is possible to disagree with Piaget's interpretations but not the accuracy of his findings.

Piaget demonstrated a lack of arrogance. In his reviews of the research of other researchers and theorists, he showed great respect for the contributions they made though he sometimes disagreed with their conclusions. And he admitted that his own thinking was not complete; that he was still learning.

I admire Piaget as a life-long learner. Publishing his first paper at age 11 and continuing to do research as a teenager, it is remarkable that he was still engaged in research the year of his death in 1980, observing in his last interview at the age of 84: "We are in the middle of our study of reason right now" (Voyat, 1980). Though Piaget did not discuss it, I suspect that his work was his play, that he thoroughly enjoyed finding answers to his lifelong questions.

CONCLUSION

So, what about child's play? Piaget has been quoted as saying "play is the work of the child" (Piaget, 1945/1962) (as have Maria Montessori and Mr. Fred Rogers). Piaget's careful research has shown that through play, children learn about the world, solve problems, and develop morally. Through his own research and his mentoring of other scholars, Piaget influenced early childhood education programs, science education, and LEGO robotics, and leaves a legacy of thought leaders and educators who, in diverse ways, have made learning more fun and more hands-on. At a time when the focus on testing and test preparation has removed much of the playfulness and creativity from learning in many public schools, Piaget's understanding of play needs reconsideration by today's educators.

REFERENCES

Bers, M. U. (2008). *Blocks to robots: Learning with technology in the early childhood classroom*. Teachers College Press.

Blikstein, P. (n.d.). Seymour Papert's legacy: Thinking about learning and learning about thinking. Transformative Learning Technologies Lab, Stanford Graduate School of Education. https://tltl.stanford.edu/content/seymour-papert-s-legacy-thinking-about-learning-and-learning-about-thinking

Britannica (2017) Jean Piaget. https://www.britannica.com/biography/Jean-Piaget

Cavicchi, E. (2006). Faraday and Piaget: Experimenting in relation with the world. *Perspectives on science, 14*(1), 66–96.

Counsell, S., Escalada, L., Geiken, R., Sander, M., Uhlenberg, J., Ven Meeteren, B., Yoshizawa, S., Zan, B. (2016). *STEM learning with young children: Inquiry teaching with ramps and pathways*. Teachers College Press.

DeVries, R., & Kohlberg, L. (1987). *Programs of early education: The constructivist view*. Longman.

DeVries, R. & Sales, C. (2011). *Ramps & pathways: A constructivist approach to physics with young children.* National Association for the Education of Young Children.

Duckworth, E. (n.d.) Biography. Retrieved from http://mohellmann.tripod.com/id1.html

Duckworth, E. (2006). *"The having of wonderful ideas" and other essays on teaching and learning* (third edition). Teachers College Press.

Herron, R. E., & Sutton-Smith, B. (1971). *Child's play*. John Wiley.

Kamii, C., & DeVries, R. (1980). *Group games in early education: Implications of Piaget's theory.* National Association for the Education of Young Children.

Kohlberg, L. (1987). *Child psychology and childhood education: A cognitive-developmental view.* Longman.

Papert, S. (1982/1993). *Mindstorms: Children, computers, and powerful ideas* (second edition). Basic Books.

Papert, S. (1993). *The children's machine: Rethinking school in the age of the computer*. Basic Books.

Piaget, J. (1918/1977). *To understand is to invent: The future of education.* Penguin Books.

Piaget, J. (1923/2009). *The language and thought of the child.* Routledge.

Piaget, J. (1926/1951). *The child's conception of physical causality.* Littlefield, Adams & Co.

Piaget, J. (1930/1972). *The child's conception of the world: A 20th-century classic of child psychology*. Littlefield Adams.

Piaget, J. (1932/1997). *The moral judgment of the child.* Free Press.

Piaget, J. (1935/1969). *Science of education and the psychology of the child.* Viking Press

Piaget, J. (1937/1954). *The construction of reality in the child.* Ballantine Books.

Piaget, J. (1941/1965). *The child's conception of number*. The Norton Library.

Piaget, J. (1945/1962). *Play, dreams and imitation in childhood.* W.W. Norton.

Piaget, J. (1962/2000). Commentary on Vygotsky's criticisms of language and thought of the child and judgement and reasoning in the child. *New Ideas in Psychology, 18*, 241–259.

Piaget, J. (1970). Piaget's theory. In P. H. Mussen (Ed.), *Carmichael's manual of child psychology, volume 1* (pp. 703–732). John Wiley & Sons, Inc.

Piaget, J. (1971). Response to Brian Sutton-Smith. In Herron, R. and Sutton-Smith, G., *Child's play* (pp. 337–339). John Wiley.

Piaget, J. (1973). How a child's mind grows. In M. Miller (Ed), *The neglected years: Early childhood* (pp. 17–36). UNICEF.

Piaget-Montessori Answers (n.d.) http://montessorianswers.com/piaget.html

Resnick, M. (2017). *Lifelong kindergarten: Cultivating creativity through projects, passion, peers, and play*. The MIT Press.

Sutton-Smith, B. (1971a). Piaget on play: A critique. In R. E. Herron and B. Sutton-Smith, *Child's play* (pp. 326–336). John Wiley.

Sutton-Smith, B. (1971b). A reply to Piaget: A play theory of copy. In Herron, R. E. and Sutton-Smith, B., *Child's play* (pp. 340–342). John Wiley.

Voyat, G. (1980, February). Interview with Jean Piaget. http://www.fondationjean-piaget.ch/fjp/site/textes/VE/JP80_Voyat_interview.pdf

Vygotsky, L. (1932). Piaget's theory of child language and thought. https://www.ufrgs.br/psicoeduc/vygotsky/piaget%E2%80%99s-theory-child-language-and-thought/

8

Lev Vygotsky

1896–1934

Joanna Cemore Brigden

Lev Vygotsky.

Play is a vehicle for learning.

"We're going to make some simple scrambled eggs, nothing could be easier" says Martha Stewart to her guest Marcia Cross, on the Martha Stewart television talk show (2017). Marcia Cross, an American actress, well known for her character Bree on *Desperate Housewives*, steps back a bit from the kitchen island and states that she is "terrified." She puts the butter in the wrong place, and is swiftly corrected by Martha. Next, she exclaims "I wasn't kidding!" and covers her mouth laughing, "I can't cook." Marcia is visibly uncomfortable until she decides, "Maybe I should just *pretend* I'm in character and I'll do better." Her character Bree on *Desperate Housewives* is somewhat of a "Martha Stewart" type of character who excels at cooking and baking. So, Martha Stewart addresses Marcia as Bree and asks about her fictional life. Marcia's demeanor immediately transforms. She is at ease, stirring the eggs and talking about her life. In a relaxed tone, she says, *I am much better now that I am acting* (Stewart, 2017).

VYGOTSKY ON PLAY

What is so magical about acting "as if" instead of just being? Is it magic or is it part of who we are and how we develop as humans that we are given this gift of pretense to allow us to be more than we believe ourselves to be? The cognitive theorist, Lev Vygotsky, who is renowned for his insights into language, thought, and play, asserted that among preschool-aged children, pretend play allows the child to function at a higher level than in other activities of childhood. According to Vygotsky (1966), a child is "always above his average age, above his daily behavior" in play (p.552).

At least two developmental factors appear to contribute to this "heads above" phenomenon. One is that the imaginary situation allows for some distance from self and gives a child a sense of freedom that staves off fear of failure because *it's not really me if I am pretending*. The second is the feeling of invincibility that preschoolers have that gives them the confidence to try new things and believe they are capable of more than they may be. Perhaps these two factors converge to create a powerful dynamic, which we identify as pretense, that produces actions and thoughts well above a child's non-play abilities (Vygotsky, 1966).

When Vygotsky (1966) speaks of play in preschoolers, he means pretense. Whereas pretense is often thought of as a type of play, he delineates play as pretense, the creation of an imaginary situation, "the leading source of development in pre-school years" (p. 537). Vygotsky (1978) asserts that play is not real life, yet "play contains all developmental tendencies in a condensed form and is itself a major source of development (p.102).

Ah, but we'd be missing what is the magic of play, the wider background, changes in needs and consciousness, creation of voluntary intentions, creating real plans, and volitional motives. These are why pretense is "the highest level of preschool development" (Vygotsky, 1978, p.102). In play activities, a child moves forward in all development, not just the narrow focus of cognition. Imaginative play is "a means of developing abstract thought" (Vygotsky, 1966, p. 553).

"Play is a transitional stage . . . at that critical moment when a stick—i.e., an object—becomes a pivot for severing the meaning of horse from a real horse" (Vygotsky, 1978, p. 546). Here, reality is altered for the child and they must have an object to orient to. "In play a child unconsciously and spontaneously makes use of the fact that he can separate meaning from an object without knowing he is doing it" (p. 548). Take for example, the previously mentioned stick as a horse or a finger to represent a person in "Where is Thumbkin?" In this song the child uses each finger to represent a person in dialogue with a finger on the other hand.

Early Play

Whereas make-believe is an imaginary situation, it derives from "a real situation" (Vygotsky, 1978, p. 103) in the child's life. Early play is then seen as a "recollection of something that has actually happened . . . more memory than a novel imaginary situation" (Vygotsky, 1978, p. 103). The way the child expands on the real situation during play is where the imagination component enters.

Early play leads to the knowing of things a child doesn't know they know. Abilities are used and meanings get separated from objects. The self-created imaginary situations consist of the child breaking free of reliance on real concrete objects and situations. Now, instead of imitating real situations, the child creates decontextualized meaning in real situations. At this age, unrealizable tendencies and desires emerge. It appears to Vygotsky that this development of tendencies and desires and the creation of these imaginary situations can come together at the same time, as if imagination were a new way of dealing with life and is a new psychological process for the child to access as needed (Vygotsky, 1966).

This freedom is then confounded by following self-imposed rules emanating from the meaning assigned to the created situation. Even though in play a child is liberated from those constraints, he still adheres to rules. Vygotsky (1966) considers play without rules to not be play at all since "the imaginary situation of any form of play already contains rules of behavior" (p. 94), since links are made between pretense and social emotional needs such as self-regulation.

Heads Above

Vygotsky (1966) recognized make-believe play for its self-regulatory value. During imaginative play the child is met with contradictory motives—to act spontaneously and to follow the rules. The child has no externally imposed rules. During play he can do whatever he wants. On the other hand, the child is under continuous "demands . . . to act against immediate impulse" (p. 548). During play, it seems that to follow the rules of the role or game gives more pleasure to the child than acting on impulse.

For example, John and Annie, two four-year-old preschool children, are pretending to be a dog and its owner. John is down on his hands and knees panting and barking. Annie goes to John and says, "What do you want, Doggy?" He continues to pant and bark, "What do you want, Doggy?" Annie tries again. John the Doggy barks again and runs over (on hands and knees) to the play cupboard. Annie says excitedly, "Oh! Do you want something to eat?" "Ruff! Ruff!" he responds. Annie pretends to set out food for the dog and John pretends to eat it. She then pets the dog and refers to him as "Good Doggy."

In this situation, John could have become frustrated when Annie did not know what he wanted. Instead of breaking the rule of his role as a dog by speaking, John continued to try to communicate his needs to Annie in a way consistent with his knowledge of dogs. In this way John acts against his immediate impulse to be understood and instead continues to act as a dog would. Thus, the interaction with Annie as a dog was more pleasurable than being understood immediately by her.

Vygotsky (1966) states, "Play continually creates demands on the child to act against immediate impulse" (p. 548). A constant internal conflict occurs during play as the child is acting against impulse without external enforcement. In each instance, the child must struggle with the choice of playing by the rules of the situation or doing what he would do if he acted spontaneously (Vygotsky, 1966).

In essence, the child is developing the skill of self-control by delaying gratification. When Cemore and Herwig (2005) studied preschoolers at play, they found that children who spent more time engaged in pretense were more likely to be able to delay gratification. Their findings build on earlier studies that linked pretense with the ability of preschool and primary children to delay gratification (Franklin, 1975; Mischel & Baker, 1975; Meichenbaum &

Goodman, 1971; Riess, 1957; Saltz, Dixon, & Johnson, 1977; Singer, 1955, 1961). Children who were reported to engage in pretense at home and report imaginary companions were also more capable of tolerating long waits and to delay gratification (Riess, 1957; Singer, 1961).

Zone of Proximal Development

The most recognizable contribution of Vygotsky (1966) is the notion of the "zone of proximal development," which he states is created through play (p. 552). The zone of proximal development is "the distance between the actual developmental level as determined by independent problem solving and the level of potential development as determined through problem solving under adult guidance or in collaboration with more capable peers" (p. 86). In this zone, where learning takes place, the learner develops an understanding of the concept or objective. The idea of the ZPD is akin to Piaget's premise that learning occurs in the state between equilibrium and disequilibrium (Piaget, 1923/2009).

Emotional Intelligence

Studies have shown a connection between pretense and components of emotional intelligence, such as emotional competence, emotional development, locus of control, affect, impulsive behavior, and delay of gratification. "If the goal is to promote social competence, emotional development, or the general well-being of the child . . . dramatic play may be an appropriate choice" (Brainerd, 1982).

Studying the effects of sociodramatic play on children's locus of control, Swink and Buchanan (1984) found evidence of emotional awareness, increased sensitivity to others, and feelings of power over the environment linked with engagement in sociodramatic play. Investigations by Singer and Singer (1981, 1990) consistently found that those children who played more imaginatively were also more likely to be scored as showing more smiling and laughing, more cooperation with teachers, and less evidence of the more negative affects such as anger, distress, or fatigue and sluggishness.

Older children who indicate greater imaginative behavior have also been shown to engage in less antisocial and/or impulsive behavior (Herskovitz, Levine, & Spivak, 1959). Impulse control and/or delay of gratification behaviors have also been shown to be related to pretend play of children (Cemore & Herwig, 2005; Franklin, 1975; Mischel & Baker, 1975; Meichenbaum & Goodman, 1971; Riess, 1957; Saltz, Dixon, & Johnson, 1977; Singer, 1955, 1961). Even with older children and early adolescents, studies have shown that those individuals who indicated greater imaginative behavior were also less likely to engage in various kinds of antisocial or impulsive behavior (Herskovitz et al., 1959).

"Through pretend play children learn to become comfortable with emotion and with affect-laden ideation. Affect content or primary process content is permitted to surface and be expressed through play" (Russ, 1998, p. 222). The cathartic experience of pretense and the practice of expressing differing emotions in a safe "play" environment may enable the child to better perceive emotions, facilitate thoughts, understand emotions, and manage emotions, all of which are the four main areas of the ability model of EI as presented by Mayer and colleagues. (2000).

Vygotskian theory is based on social interactions in which make-believe play is predominantly a social activity. In contrast, Piaget emphasizes a spontaneous emergence of play that incorporates social interactions. Today make-believe play is commonly seen as both a social activity and a solitary activity of preschool children, which fits well with Vygotsky's perspective. Vygotsky (1966) asserts that children satisfy certain needs and incentives in play. This can be achieved through either solitary or social make-believe play. Solitary play used to have a negative connotation. Although earlier research linked solitary play to anti-social behaviors and other negative outcomes, that view is beginning to change. In one such study, Cemore and Herwig (2005) found that there was no difference in children's ability to delay gratification (one of the defining skills of emotional intelligence) if their time engaged in pretense was spent alone or if it was spent with others. The rules of the role apply whether children are delaying their gratification during play with others or in solitude.

Creativity

Creative abilities and imaginative play have been shown to carry an influence into the elementary years (Russ, 1993; Russ, Robins, & Christiano, 1999; Shmukler, 1982–83). Litt (1973) found that ten-year-old children during an interview showing more current evidence of persistent imaginative play scored higher on creative fluency or divergent production. Dansky and Silverman (1973) found preschool children's associative fluency and divergent thought processes were strengthened by imaginatively focused play training. In later work, Dansky and Silverman (1973) put forward the suggestion that pretense establishes a way of thought and action, a way of looking at things in the world that creates more creative thinking in other settings. Pretend play may be a way for children to learn new information more efficiently than cognitive training.

Russ and Grossman-McKee (1990) provided evidence of a consistent link between children's fantasy play and more divergent thought processes or creativity on the Rorschach Ink Blots. In a series of studies, Wyver and Spence (1999) found that not only does training in pretense effect divergent problem solving but that training in divergent problem solving increased some kinds of pretend play.

Naturalistic observation studies have also shown a significant association between pretense and divergent problem solving. Johnson (1976) found pretend play of three- to five-year-old children to be significantly correlated with semantic divergent problem-solving skills if the pretend play was social.

The Child's Right to Play

Motivation is central to learning. It seems that, in this age of accountability, motivation to learn would be a high priority. By emphasizing the motivational aspect of play, which teachers already acknowledge as central to learning, administrators could make play more palatable in an age of accountability and achievement. A playful approach could, in turn, provide play with the respect it so rightly deserves. This would also help teachers communicate with parents about the rigors and joys of play for their child's school and personal success.

Public schools have faced increasing pressure in recent years to emphasize direct instruction and focus on objective measures of achievement. This shift has resulted in debate among developmental scientists concerning the effects of these changes on children's creative thinking abilities, social-emotional development, and achievement. With this emphasis on achievement, administrators seek to achieve standardized test scores and objectives that were created by folks distant from the actual students. As a result, children have less time to play and fewer playful ways of learning, despite the fact that research provides evidence of positive outcomes related to recess, outdoor play, and playful teaching (Jarrett, 2013).

CONCLUSION

The Russian psychologist Lev Vygotsky, who is heralded as one of the most influential cognitive theorists of the twentieth century, has contributed greatly to our understandings of children's play. He promoted the idea that, during play, children are capable of more and perform "heads above" their normal level. He emphasized that children want to learn and are eager to engage in activities related to their interests. Pretend play hits all of these points by motivating students, which leads to learning, achievement, and innovation.

REFERENCES

Brainerd, C. J. (1982). Effects of group and individualized dramatic play training on cognitive development. *Contributions to Human Development, 6,* 128.

Cemore, J. J., & Herwig, J. (2005). Delay of gratification and make-believe play of preschoolers. *Journal of Research in Childhood Education, 19*, 3, 251–266.

Dansky, J., & Silverman, I. (1973). Effects of play on associative fluency in preschool-aged children, *Developmental Psychology, 9,* 38–43.

Franklin, D. (1975). Block play modeling and its relationship to imaginativeness, impulsivity, reflection, and internal-external control. Predissertation Master's research, Yale University.

Herskovitz, H., Levine, M., & Spivak, G. (1959). Anti-social behavior of adolescents from higher socioeconomic groups. *Journal of Nervous and Mental Diseases, 125,* 467–476.

Jarrett, O. (2013). A research-based case for recess. US Play Coalition.Clemson.edu

Johnson, J. E. (1976). Relations of divergent thinking and intelligence test scores with social and nonsocial make-believe play of preschool children. *Child Development, 47,*1200–1203.

Litt, H. (1973). Imagery in children's thinking. Doctoral dissertation. Liverpool University.

Mayer, J. D., Salovey, P., & Caruso, D. (2000). Emotional intelligence as *zeitgeist,* as personality, and as a mental ability. In R. Bar-On and J. D. A. Parker (Eds.), *Handbook of emotional intelligence.* Jossey-Bass.

Meichenbaum, D., & Goodman, J. (1971). Training impulsive children to talk to themselves. *Journal of Abnormal Psychology, 77,* 115–121.

Mischel, W., & Baker, N. (1975). Cognitive transformation of reward objects through instructions. *Journal of Personality and Social Psychology, 31,* 254–261.

Piaget, J. (1923/2009). *The language and thought of the child.* Routledge.

Riess, A. (1957). A study of some genetic behavioral correlates of human movement responses in children's Rorschach protocols. Unpublished doctoral dissertation, New York University.

Russ, S. W. (1993). *Affect and creativity: The role of affect and play in the creative process.* Lawrence Erlbaum Associations, Inc.

Russ, S. W. (1998). The impact of repression on creativity. *Psychological Inquiry, 9,* 221–223.

Russ, S. W., & Grossman-McKee, A. (1990). Affective expression in children's fantasy play, primary process thinking on the Rorschach and divergent thinking. *Journal of Personality Assessment, 54,* 756–771.

Russ, S. W., Robins, A. L., & Christiano, B. A. (1999). Pretend Play: Longitudinal prediction of creativity and affect in fantasy in children. *Creativity Research Journal, 12,* 129–139.

Saltz, E., Dixon, D., & Johnson, J. (1977). Training disadvantaged preschoolers on various fantasy activities: Effects on cognitive functioning and impulse control. *Child Development, 46,* 367–380.

Shmukler, D. (1982-83). Preschool imaginative play and its relationship to subsequent third grade assessment. *Imagination, Cognition and Personality, 2,* 231–240.

Singer, J. L. (1955). Delayed gratification and ego development: Implications for clinical and experimental research. *Journal of Consulting Psychology, 19,* 259–266.

Singer, J. L. (1961). Imagination and waiting ability in young children. *Journal of Personality, 29,* 396–413.

Singer, J. L., & Singer, D. G. (1981). *Television, imagination and aggression: A study of preschoolers*. Erlbaum.

Singer, D. G., & Singer, J. L. (1990). *The house of make-believe: Children's play and the developing imagination.* Harvard University Press.

Stewart, M. (Writer), & Burnett, M. (Director). (2017, July 9th). "Marcia Cross talks Desperate Housewives with Martha Stewart." *The Martha Stewart Show.* Mark Burnett Productions.

Swink, D. F., & Buchanan, R. (1984). The effects of sociodramatic goal-oriented play and non-goal-oriented role play on locus of control. *Journal of Clinical Psychology, 40,* 1178–1183.

Vygotsky, L. S. (1966). Play and its role in the mental development of the child. *Soviet Psychology 12*, *6,* 62–76.

Vygotsky, L. S. (1978). *Mind in society: The development of higher psychological processes.* Harvard University Press.

Wyver, S. R., & Spence, S. H. (1999). Play and divergent problem solving: Evidence supporting a reciprocal relationship. *Early Education and Development, 10,* 419–444.

9

Urie Bronfenbrenner

1917–2005

Debra Lawrence

Urie Bronfenbrenner.

Play is important to social development.

Urie Bronfenbrenner was a developmental psychologist and professor who played an instrumental role in the formation of Head Start. Born in Russia in 1917, Urie Bronfenbrenner moved stateside with his family at the age of six and the duality between the Russian culture of his childhood and his American upbringing is evident in his work as a social scientist and author. Deeply influenced by his father, a neuropathologist, who taught him about the functional interdependence of life systems, he studied the role of the environment in human development and created the ecological systems theory (Bronfenbrenner, 1979, p. xii).

BRONFENBRENNER AND HEAD START

Although he was an influential Cornell scholar, Bronfenbrenner is perhaps best known as a co-founder of Head Start. In 1964, when President Lyndon Johnson declared a War on Poverty, he gathered a committee to deliberate the issues. One member, Urie Bronfenbrenner, testified before Congress in favor of the proposed antipoverty bill and spoke of the effects of environment on young developing minds. Prior to his testimony, the consensus among members of Congress was that children born in poverty are inherently less intelligent and low achievement was inevitable due to genetics. However, Urie Bronfenbrenner challenged their deficit perspective and argued that a program of early enrichment could result in beneficial outcomes (Woo, 2005).

Afterwards, Bronfenbrenner received an invitation to have tea with the First Lady at the White House, where Lady Bird Johnson sought his input about early childhood education. Next, Urie Bronfenbrenner was appointed to a federal panel to design a nationwide program for the purpose of promoting school readiness for children in poverty. Since its inception in 1965, the federally funded Head Start program has served over 20 million families (Woo, 2005).

Ecological Systems Theory

Urie Bronfenbrenner developed a theory, the Ecological Systems Theory, in which he offered a conceptual framework for perceiving human development. In this view, social development begins with the child at the center and evolves with subsequent inter-related systems forming rings of impact in expanding circles around the child. His description of these concentric levels, which is analogous to the Russian nesting dolls of his homeland, proposes that human development is layered within multiple contexts (Bronfenbrenner, 1979).

Bronfenbrenner viewed the child as developing within a complex system of relationships affected by multiple levels of the surrounding environment, as well as the complex systems that are identified as factors of nature and nurture. *Nature* includes the unique biology of each child and includes gender and genetic makeup. *Nurture* consists of the child's experiences, such as prenatal and life experiences, level of bonding and attachment, temperament, health, and supports within each of the expanding systems. Another facet of Bronfenbrenner's theory is its bi-directional impact, which means that the child impacts each of the systems, even as the systems affect the child's development (Lawrence, 2013).

When Urie Bronfenbrenner developed the Ecological Systems Theory, he wanted to portray child development from the innermost to the outermost as well as through the lens of cultural values, beliefs, and experiences. In his original descriptions of the levels of societal impact—the micro, meso, exo, and maxo—he addressed the importance of context and highlighted the wider economic, political, and cultural factors that influence the lives of children. Additionally, Bronfenbrenner clarified that the unique biology of each child will influence their response to the environment and impact development and learning (Lawrence, 2013).

Levels of the Ecological Systems

Microsystem. In the first level of the ecological system, the microsystem, the members have direct contact with a child. They are the individuals such as family, teachers, peers, and neighbors who interact with the child on a daily or weekly basis. The close relationships are bi-directional, meaning that their input has an impact on the child and the child likewise can influence them. It is the first and smallest circle of influence (Bronfenbrenner, 1979).

Mesosystem. The next level of Bronfenbrenner's expanding social system is known as the mesosystem. It includes the relationships with the individuals in the microsystem as well as others who are close to the child and can be seen as a system of microsystems. For example, a child's teacher is part of the mesosystem. Other possibilities include neighbors, extended family, and members of their faith community (Bronfenbrenner, 1979).

Exosystem. Branching out, the exosystem can include members of the microsystem and the mesosystem, but these individuals may not have regular contact with the child. Examples of exosystem members include parents' colleagues, distant relatives, family friends, and people who represent community social services or health services, such as the family doctor. Members of the exosystem can affect the child primarily by impacting members of their microsystem, such as supporting the family during a difficult time or the reverse—having a detrimental impact on a family member, which will affect the child (Bronfenbrenner, 1979).

Macrosystem. The macrosystem pertains to national policies, laws, resources, and cultural values. The society at large may provide for the children within it, but cultural norms can serve as barriers to providing adequate support to families. Thus, countries that provide adequate services to all of the members will have better education, health care, and provisions for parental leave than nations that lack these support systems (Bronfenbrenner, 1979).

Chronosystem. The chronosystem encompasses all of the previous systems as well as an overarching perspective of all of the environmental influences that can occur during the life of a child. The changes can include birth, death, housing adjustments, immigration policies, violence, discrimination, divorce, incarceration, and trauma-related events such as school shootings, war, accidents, natural disasters, and other calamities (Bronfenbrenner & Ceci, 1994).

Bronfenbrenner on Play

In his perennial quest to understand the complexities of human development, Urie Bronfenbrenner embarked on a project to explore childhood from a cross-cultural perspective. He and his colleagues visited the United Soviet Socialist Republic on several occasions during the 1960s to collect data in the form of observations, interviews, photographs, and notes from visits to nursery schools and elementary schools. As a result of these efforts, Bronfenbrenner and his co-author, John Condry, produced a book, *Two Worlds of Childhood: U.S. and U.S.S.R,* that portrays similarities and contrasts from these cultures (Bronfenbrenner & Condry, 1970).

Among the notes on childhood from the two countries are numerous references to the ways that children play in each culture. Although Bronfenbrenner did not emphasize the topic of play as an objective of the study, he did discuss play in the context of social development for different age groups. Bronfenbrenner described play and playful activities as part of the larger social context of the developing child. Furthermore, he provided examples of play in each of the concentric levels of the sociological circles (Bronfenbrenner & Condry, 1970).

When describing the micro level, Bronfenbrenner represented the interactions of the caregivers, or upbringers, as essential to social development through their role in playful activities. He explained how they could encourage young children to engage with adults by offering toys and bells just out of reach so that the little ones would reach for them and babble their requests. Bronfenbrenner and Condry (1970) relate how upbringers facilitated language development by engaging in serve and return verbal interactions and cultivated positive relationships with consistent sensorimotor stimulation (p. 17).

In a microsystem, the family's culture plays a vital role in a child's development, so the cultural values and beliefs within the child's home, family, and community all influence how children view themselves and their relationships. Bronfenbrenner's views on play in the microsystem were in alignment with his ecological systems view, which were "influenced by Vygotsky, who viewed play as important to social development" (Bronfenbrenner, 1979, p. 52)

As children grow, they are influenced more by peers, so they tend to expand beyond their microsystem for play, into the mesosystem level. In this social milieu, the Russian children in Bronfenbrenner's study participated in playful activities with their neighbors as comrades, and were often observed in mixed age groups (Bronfenbrenner & Condry, 1970, p. 29). From the perspective of the ecological systems theory, play in the mesosystem will include friends from school, church, and many other community organizations such as Scouts, sport teams, and clubs (Bronfenbrenner, 1979).

The play in both the U.S.A. and U.S.S.R. that occurred within the social level known as the exosystem covered a broader geographical range. Bronfenbrenner and Condry (1970) observed that older Russian children taught games to younger children in their villages and they referred to it as group adoption (p. 50). Similarly, during the era in which the book was written, the authors determined that American children often had full run of their neighborhoods and were able to engage in active participation in adult life (Bronfenbrenner & Condry, 1970, p. 96). However, Bronfenbrenner lamented the fact that many American children had to travel in a car to reach their destination for play as part of a team (Bronfenbrenner & Condry, 1970, p. 97).

At the next social level, the macrosystem, play is influenced by facilities that are provided by their country such as playgrounds, parks, and the policies that protect them. Furthermore, the personnel that provide maintenance and protection of the facilities can be considered part of the macrosystem of opportunities for play (Bronfenbrenner, 1979).

From the perspective of the chronosystem, many events in the life of a child will have an impact on their opportunities to play, choice of playmates, and freedom to choose play activities. However, throughout all of the changes in the life of a child, play will remain and serve as an important part of their growth and development (Bronfenbrenner & Condry, 1970; Bronfenbrenner & Condry, 1994).

The Child's Right to Play

How does Bronfenbrenner inform our understanding of the child's right to play?

First of all, when looking at the microsystem of social development, there are several factors to consider about play. Parents must consider the safety of the immediate surroundings, how the family's work schedule can facilitate opportunities for play, whether they can allow children to play unsupervised in their neighborhood, or if the decline of recess during the school day has diminished time for free play. Furthermore, parents often believe that ancillary activities such as sports, dance, tutoring, or other structured recreation activities are more important than freedom to play without adult direction (Jarrett, 2013).

In the mesosystem, the parents' employers might influence play since work conditions can influence home life. For example, a parent who must work late hours may not be able to provide their child with time to play in the neighborhood before bedtime. So, even though the child does not interact directly with the work colleagues, their decisions can influence the family schedule and, in turn, restrict time for unstructured play (Bronfenbrenner, 1979).

From the perspective of the macrosystem, cultures that value child play will provide abundant opportunities for children to engage in play in public places.

> Facilities such as parks, playgrounds, zoos, and children's museums are more prevalent in communities that prioritize family values and the needs of children, especially play (Bronfenbrenner, 1979).

Lastly, since the events in the chronosystem are unique to the child and family, there will be variables in regard to the right to play. A sibling born with a disability or an aging relative at home might limit the child's play time. Frequent moves by the family can also limit the child's ability to form friendships or have access to areas for play. If a child has experienced a traumatic event, they may be less inclined to play (Bronfenbrenner, 1995).

CONCLUSION

As a nation, we must recognize the importance of the healthy development of each child, which includes the right to play. The future of our democracy hinges on our ability to ensure that we provide support to children and their families. The choices made, the way public dollars are invested, the policies and laws that are created are all representative of the nation's priorities. In future decades, the United States will be judged on whether its emphasis was on supporting a child's development or whether its focus on policies and funding were misplaced. In the words of Urie Bronfenbrenner,

> *We as a nation need to be re-educated about the necessary and sufficient conditions for making human beings human. We need to be re-educated not as parents—but as workers, neighbors, and friends; and as members of the organizations, committees, boards—and, especially, the informal networks that control our social institutions and thereby determine the conditions of life for our families and their children.* (Bronfenbrenner, 2004)

REFERENCES

Bronfenbrenner, U. (1979). *The ecology of human development: Experiments by nature and design.* Harvard University Press.

Bronfenbrenner, U. (1995). Developmental ecology through space and time: A future perspective. In *Examining lives in context: Perspectives on the ecology of human development,* American Psychological Association, Washington DC, 619-648. https://doi.org/10.1037/10176-018

Bronfenbrenner, U. (ed.) (2004). *Making human beings human: Bioecological perspectives on human development.* Sage Publications.

Bronfenbrenner, U., & Ceci, S. J. (1994). Nature-nurture reconceptualised: A bioecological model. *Psychological Review, 10*, 4, 568–586.

Bronfenbrenner, U., & Condry, J. (1970). *Two worlds of childhood: U.S. and U.S.S.R.* George Allen & Unwin, LTD.

Jarrett, O. (2013). A research-based case for recess. US Play Coalition.Clemson.edu

Lawrence, D. (2013). Social and emotional development. In *Learning from Head Start.* Edited by S. W. Gifford. Rowman & Littlefield.

Woo, E. (2005). Obituary: Urie Bronfenbrenner: Theories altered approach to child development. *Los Angeles Times.*

10

Sara Smilansky

1922–2006

Karen Walker and Shelley Harris

Sara Smilansky.

Sociodramatic play activates resources that stimulate emotional, social, and intellectual growth in the child, which in turn affects the child's success in school.

Child therapists and students of play benefit from the work of Sara Smilansky, who provided significant contributions to our collective knowledge of the role of play in children's learning, language, and expressions of grief. In her prolific body of work, she explored many topics in child development such as play, a study of the experiences of twins, the role of affective skills in learning, and how to help children cope with grief caused by losses such as death and divorce (Smilansky, 1987; Smilansky & Shefatya, 1990; Smilansky, 1992a; Smilansky, 1992b). Smilansky enhanced our understandings of children's thought processes during play and provided guidance on how to facilitate socio-emotional, cognitive, and academic development with playful interventions (Smilansky & Shefatya, 1990). She conducted research on the effects of sociodramatic play and advocated for it as a therapeutic medium with children from a diverse spectrum of socioeconomic and cultural backgrounds in both the United States and Israel (Smilansky, 1968). Additionally, Smilansky is noted for her work with the renowned Swiss psychologist, Jean Piaget and their collaboration on categories of play (Piaget, 1962).

PROFILE OF SMILANSKY

Born in Israel in 1922, Sara Smilansky traveled abroad to pursue her studies and completed a doctorate at Ohio State University. She began her academic career as a professor at Tel Aviv University and also served as a visiting professor in the United States, at Ohio State University and the University of Maryland. Smilansky influenced the realm of play therapy with research and publications on children in poverty, the effect of trauma on children, and how children express their inner thoughts during sociodramatic play (Han, 2016).

Research on Play with Disadvantaged Children

In the 1960s, Sara Smilansky led a research project in Jerusalem to explore therapeutic methods for helping children from the socioculturally underprivileged strata (Smilansky, 1968). Under her supervision, five field workers orchestrated play sessions in thirty-six classrooms with children from the ages of three to six years old. In eighteen of the classrooms, the students were identified as having middle and high sociocultural backgrounds. In the experimental group, the students were primarily children from immigrant families from Middle Eastern and North African countries. The researchers categorized the groups based on characteristics such as their home country, number of children in the family, parents' education level, and parents' occupations. The overarching purpose of the study was to determine how interventions in the form of intentional scaffolding during sociodramatic play sessions could enhance development and facilitate school readiness (Smilansky, 1968).

Smilansky observed that the children in the control group lacked the ability to fully concentrate and control their behavior long enough to engage in sociodramatic play. She theorized that by implementing carefully planned sociodramatic play sessions, her team of play tutors could facilitate healing for these students. The objective was to determine whether offering opportunities for students to ameliorate their traumatic experiences could help them organize their scattered thoughts and transform their incomplete cognitive skills into new conceptual schemes. Smilansky (1968) shared her findings in *The Effects of Sociodramatic Play on Disadvantaged Preschool Children,* which portrayed sociodramatic play as a means to facilitate the development of social, cognitive, and language skills, and to promote healing. Later, she expanded her research to investigate how drawing with children can effectively promote the development of cognitive skills (Mooney & Smilansky, 1973).

Stages of Play: Piaget

In 1962, Jean Piaget shifted his focus on play. Whereas in the past he had highlighted the role of play in social and emotional development, his thinking evolved to encompass an even greater emphasis on the role of play in cognitive development. Piaget theorized that children assimilated or accommodated information into their schema during play, which contributed to learning. For example, young children might refer to a dog as a cat, when they encounter a furry four-legged creature. As the parent enlightens them to the fact that it is, in fact, a small dog, children will assimilate this information to the new meaning, and then accommodate it into their schema about animals. Thus, Piaget portrays how assimilation and accommodation during play reflect cognitive processes. Piaget collaborated with Smilansky to develop a theory about three stages of play, which was represented in a chronological sequence:

- **Sensory play**. Babies and children up to two years of age are in the sensorimotor stage of cognitive development and learn by using their senses to explore objects.

- **Symbolic play**. Young children between the ages of two and seven, the pre-operational stage of cognitive development, learn by engaging in symbolic play.
- **Games with rules**. Children between the ages of seven and eleven, which is the concrete operational stage of cognitive development, become interested in participating in games with rules. (Piaget, 1962)

Stages of Play: Smilansky

Smilansky continued to cultivate the concept of stages of play and, along with her colleague, Leah Shefatya, developed another theory about the categories of play. In their revised list, they added another category, described play as having more fluidity, and did not specify ages for each type of play:

> **Functional play.** Children explore and manipulate toys and objects.
>
> **Constructive play.** Children use materials to plan new creations.
>
> **Games with rules.** Children engage in activities that involve rules, either prearranged or made up during the play activity.
>
> **Dramatic play.** Children explore new roles as they engage in make-believe activities.
>
> (Smilansky & Shefatya, 1990)

Facilitating Play

In response to a 1987 survey, which indicated that early childhood educators were ambivalent about classroom play, Sara Smilansky and Leah Shefatya (1990) explored ways to guide play activities and collaborated on the book, *Facilitating Play: A Medium for Promoting Cognitive, Socio-Emotional, and Academic Development in Young Children.* Smilansky was especially interested in sociodramatic play because she deemed it "one of the most fascinating phenomena of early childhood. It consists of complex behavior, characterized by joyful concentration, intensity, and expressive fluency" (Smilansky & Shefatya, 1990, p. xi). Early in her career, Smilansky had defined the phenomena of sociodramatic play as "a form of voluntary social play activity in which preschool children participate" (Smilansky, 1968, p. 7).

Smilansky and Shefatya (1990) discovered that kindergarten teachers assumed that "children would learn to play on their own" (p. 262) and were not prepared to facilitate play. They sought to counteract this misconception by describing how to facilitate play. By paying close attention and by watching their actions and listening to their conversations, keen observers can interpret children's thought processes. Next, they can utilize these insights to guide play interventions. Smilansky and Shefatya (1990) provide numerous examples of play episodes that illuminate children's thinking while they are immersed in their imaginative scenarios and offer guidance for advancing their play abilities.

Sociodramatic Play

After years of studying play, Smilansky and Shefatya (1990) noted, "the child participating in sociodramatic play profits simultaneously by being actor, observer, and inter-actor" (p. 34). They proposed six elements that must be present in sociodramatic play: imitative role play, make-believe in regard to objects, make-believe in regard to actions and situations, persistence, interaction, and verbal communication.

- **Imitative role play**. Children pretend to be someone or something else.
- **Make-believe in regard to objects**. Children use real or imagined objects as play props. When children are in pretend mode, they create images in their minds and use symbols to represent objects.
- **Make-believe in regard to actions and situations**. Children choose a theme for play and verbal descriptions explain actions and situations. Even actions become objects.
- **Persistence**. In order to obtain the benefits of sociodramatic play, children need to have uninterrupted blocks of time to play. When they are allowed to engage in deeper involvement, their self-made stories become more complex, thus facilitating their capacity for imagination.
- **Interaction**. When two or more children are involved in a play episode, they will interact with verbal and nonverbal communication. Together they can plan scenarios, negotiate roles, and act out their agreed roles.
- **Verbal communication**. As children interact and exchange ideas, they are enlarging their communication skills and language usage by giving cues and negotiating roles and rules. In her studies, Smilansky found that children use their most expansive vocabulary during sociodramatic play (Smilansky & Shefatya, 1990, p. 9).

Helping Children Cope with Loss

As part of her extensive research on child development, Sara Smilansky endeavored to enhance our understanding of the ways that children cope with loss and to provide guidance for parents, educators, and play therapists for the sake of equipping them with methods for assisting bereaved children. Although children must acknowledge the fact that death is part of the life cycle, they have a difficult time comprehending the irreversibility of death.

In her book, *On Death: Helping Children Understand and Cope,* Smilansky provides insights into the mourning process and offers suggestions for helping children adjust to the loss (Smilansky, 1987).

Similarly, in 1992, Sara Smilansky published another book that addresses loss, in the form of the dissolution of a child's family structure. In *Children of Divorce: The Roles of Family and School,* Smilansky (1992a) recommends specialized training as well as actively planned adult interventions to help parents, educators, and play therapists interpret how children express their grief during play and guide them toward an acceptance of the loss (p. 85).

Role of the Teacher

Perceptions of sociodramatic play along with prevailing beliefs about the teacher's role have evolved, in part, due to Smilansky's efforts to illuminate the importance of this type of play (Christie, 1985). Prior to the publication of her work on play with disadvantaged children, the literature on play intervention was scarce and attention to the topic in teacher preparation programs was minimal (Klugman & Smilansky, 1990). During this time, teachers were expected to provide props in order to set the stage for play but not to participate in the activities (Spodek, 1974). Thus, Smilansky endeavored to transform the perspective of sociodramatic play as well as describe methods for facilitating play with a variety of props and activities such as art and claywork (Hereford, Schall, & Smilansky, 1992; Smilansky, Hagan, & Lewis, 1988).

CONCLUSION

Sara Smilansky contributed to the study of child development by sharing the results of her extensive research on play. She provided insights into the ways that children communicate through play and stated that, with appropriate preparation, teachers can facilitate healing from trauma with guided play activities. Most of all, Smilansky contributed to our understanding of sociodramatic play and how it can have an effect on academic success in school. By highlighting the role of play as a medium for learning and healing, she has inspired a plethora of researchers, teachers, play therapists, and parents to utilize the medium of play.

REFERENCES

Christie, J. (1985). Training of symbolic play. *Early Child Development and Care, 19,* 43–52.

Han, M. (2016). Sociodramatic play and Sara Smilansky. In D. Couchenour & J. K. Chrisman (Eds.), *The SAGE encyclopedia of contemporary early childhood education* (1261–1263). SAGE Publications, Inc.

Hereford, N., Schall, S., & Smilansky, S. (1992). *Dramatic play: A practical guide for teaching young children.* Scholastic, Inc.

Klugman, E., & Smilansky, S. (1990). *Children's play and learning: Perspectives and policy implications.* Teachers College Press.

Mooney, R., & Smilansky, S. (1973) An experiment in the use of drawing to promote cognitive development in disadvantaged preschool children in Israel and the United States. National Center for Educational Research and Development.

Piaget, J. (1962). *Play, dreams, and imitation in childhood.* W.W. Norton & Co.

Smilansky, S. (1968). *The effects of sociodramatic play on disadvantaged preschool children.* John Wiley & Sons, Inc.

Smilansky, S. (1987). *On death: Helping children understand and cope.* Peter Lang Publishing, Inc.

Smilansky, S., Hagan, J., & Lewis, H. (1988). *Clay in the classroom: Helping children develop cognitive and affective skills for learning.* Teachers College Press.

Smilansky, S., & Shefatya, L. (1990). *Facilitating play: A medium for promoting cognitive, socio-emotional, and academic development in young children.* Psychosocial & Education Publications.

Smilansky, S. (1992a). *Children of divorce: The roles of family and school.* BJE Press.

Smilansky, S. (1992b). *Twins and their development: The roles of family and school.* BJE Press.

11

Brian Sutton-Smith

1924–2015

Walter Drew

Brian Sutton-Smith.

Play was always intended to serve a healing function whether for child or adult, making it more worthwhile to defy the depressing and dangerous aspects of life.

We practice in variable forms what we have studied and know from experience. Along the way we learn new things, new ways of thinking about what we know and how we practice. We align ourselves with theories and practices that enlighten and support our best thinking. This is what happens through exploring the illuminating play research, play theory, and play writing of Brian Sutton-Smith.

AN INFLUENTIAL SCHOLAR OF PLAY

On September 27, 2007, during the Florida Association for the Education of Young Children 50th Annual Conference, Brian Sutton-Smith presented a lecture titled *Play as the Survival Source of Optimism and Origination (The Double O)*. The heart of his message is that play and art making are expressive experiences that generate optimism about life in this world. Play generates positive feelings and energy that help us overcome emotional distress in order to survive and thrive. In play and art making, we generate original ways of allaying boredom, pessimism, and depression. The variable forms of play facilitate resilience and positive adaptation. During the play state, the experience of fun promotes resourcefulness that assists adaptive efficacy during developmental growth and life changes. The central theme in all of Brian Sutton-Smith's epic foundational research and prolific writing is that play generates *optimism and origination*, the conditions paramount to survival and healthy adaptive response across the lifespan (Sutton-Smith, 2008).

Brian Sutton-Smith has had a profound influence on interdisciplinary play research and theory construction around the world. He is one of the foremost play scholars of the last century. With more than 50 books about play, 350 scholarly articles, as well as the numerous speeches and papers he presented, Sutton-Smith was the consummate play theorist. He dedicated over 60 years of his life to research about play from an interdisciplinary perspective (Brown & Patte, 2012).

Emphasis on Free Play

Sutton-Smith was a tireless advocate of play, especially of allowing children freedom to play on their own terms without the controlling influence of adults (Sutton-Smith, 2001). He observed that most advocates promote play for discovery and skill development and argued that, while play may serve those purposes, imposing external goals denies its evolutionary function. He promoted play as a means of expressing and interpreting feelings and thoughts, not primarily as a way of representing reality. He asserted that play is about representing emotions as a part of the large-scale cultural contexts in which they occur (Sutton-Smith, 2001).

Furthermore, Sutton-Smith theorized that play is genetically designed as a biological process contributing to the healthy well-being and survival of children and adults. The main focus of education advocacy in Sutton-Smith's era, which still persists today, was a strong interest in teaching children the three "R" subjects—reading, writing and arithmetic—in order that they learn to become puritanically cultured work servants. Sutton-Smith felt passionate about questioning these work ethic attitudes that disregarded the important process of play. He saw play as a necessary cultural challenge to this view that did not charm the conventional proponents of education (Sutton-Smith, 2001). If we are to be practical advocates of play, what should we do? What are the appropriate pragmatic strategies for dealing with ambiguities in our current system?

Ambiguity of Play

As a partial response to those concerns, Sutton-Smith set out to define, organize, and clarify the multiple forms and interdisciplinary rhetorical functions of play. He collected many categories of play, such as solitary play, mind play, playful behaviors, informal social play, various audience play, performance play, celebrations and festivals, and risky or deep play. In all there were 308 different types of play, which he described as rhetorics of play in his book, *The Ambiguity of Play* (Sutton-Smith, 2001).

Seven Rhetorics of Play

Sutton-Smith attributes the development of the rhetorics to his twenty-year membership in The Association for the Study of Play (TASP), where he was also a founding member. By attending the annual conference of TASP, he became friends with other play researchers and theorists from different disciplines—such as anthropologists, folklorists, sociologists, psychologists, historians, zoologists, philosophers, artists, biologists, early childhood educators, and play therapists, each discipline having its own scholarly way of viewing play. According to Sutton-Smith, the rhetorics represent the major forms that people use to persuasively convey their preferred scholarly perspective on play. He condensed the rhetorics into seven categories: *progress, fate, power, identity, frivolity, imaginary, and self* (Brown & Patte, 2012).

Play as a Form of Progress. Play as progress embraces the idea that humans and other animals develop through play. Early childhood educators view play as a process that simultaneously synthesizes cognitive and affective input. The central point is that play is an approach to learning that strengthens academic performance, rather than only an enjoyable evolutionary experience (Sutton-Smith, 2001).

Children's play fantasies are not meant only to replicate the world. Their play is not merely a representation of everyday real events, so much as it is based on fantasy of emotional events. The logic of play lies in dealing with emotions such as *despair, anger, fear, approval, love, happiness* and how these may be expressed (Sutton-Smith, 2001).

Play as Fate. Whereas the sacred rites of primitive culture reflect play and the power of fate, modern examples include playing cards, the lottery, and rolling the dice. Since ancient times, cultures have been concerned with the rhetoric of fate and using superstition, incantations, magic, and sacrifice as a means of appealing to the power of the gods, astrological influences, or other powerful, mysterious external forces affecting us beyond our control. The belief in fate originates not in our autonomy but rather within existential optimism (Sutton-Smith, 2001).

Play as an Exercise in Power. The rhetoric of power involves rivalry and contests as a way of experiencing, expressing, and exerting power upon another individual or group. When empowered, people feel more alive, competent, and hopeful by creating and transcending ordinary reality into a more exciting alternate world. Play theory suggests that, when children play, they may compensate for the deprivation and disempowerment they experience in life. Play can give them a way of being autonomous, of empowering themselves and mastering circumstances by constructing social situations in which they are in control. Power is strengthened by forming and maintaining alliances, teams, tribes, or other groups that serve to empower and strengthen identity. Thus, play not only assuages conflict, it can also increase social adjustment. As a temporary buffer, play helps humans transcend the circumstances of reality (Sutton-Smith, 2001).

Play as a Claim for Identity. The rhetoric of identity pertains to a sense of belonging. We enjoy being playful within a collective social celebration. We need friends, colleagues, and allies with whom we associate and share the value of community. We participate in celebrations of unity at yearly conferences, parades, and festivals that renew communal identity. The playful social antics of colleagues during conventions or political conventions project energy and solidarity interpreted in terms of identity and power. The World Olympics as a contest brings together people of many nations to enjoy the play of pageantry as mass spectacle, patriotic allegiance, and enthusiasm as a means of maintaining morale and identity (Sutton-Smith, 2001).

Within the collective community of practice, we create roles, project ideas, and revel in fantasy within the chosen culture whose validation sustains us. Just as with children who play and share within the culture of the classroom, when we attend the International Play Association (IPA/USA) or The Association for the Study of Play (TASP) conferences we play and share within the culture of professional organizations that shape and strengthen identities.

Play as an Expression of Frivolity. Frivolity permits the play of extremes. Frivolously acting foolish or silly, being a little quirky or jesting beyond normal limits, affords expression in yet another play form. Some people say play is too frivolous and deny the important role it plays in human development, while others proclaim there is nothing frivolous about play, believing it is an essential evolutionary process, a time to observe and understand underlying concerns expressed through play. Treating all play as frivolousness, as something to be put aside, illustrates and adds momentum to the idea that adults should organize the kind of play through which children are believed to develop properly (Sutton-Smith, 2001).

Play as only frivolous asserts an unfortunate influence on teachers, convincing them that play is wasteful and there are more important concerns that demand time and attention. Many teachers and parents fail to accept or make time for children to become more autonomous and cooperative social beings. Viewing play as frivolity denies children time for innovating and recreating their own play society in which they can express their feelings and emotional response about reality. These are not direct expressions of reality itself but rather the inner felt concerns. Play is a tool affording practice in real-life adaptive skills to insure emotional balance and a sense of self-efficacy. The openness of frivolous play offers a unique opportunity for observing and improving social adjustment, a way of reducing social conflict, as well as mediating personal conflict within and between members of a social group (Sutton-Smith, 2001).

Imaginary Play as a Tool for Transformation. Universally, children and adults experience imaginative fantasy play. The mind imagines an ever changing stream of images, ideas, or events as an inner dialogue. Similar to a movie, stage performance, or festival, the various characters of our mind act out endless play scenarios as folly or serious, hilarious projections, frolics in fantasy, or deep concerns. Within our inner life of play fantasies, we view, respond, and often act out feelings, conflicts, and ideas as they enter into our consciousness. Compared with children, adults are more restricted imaginatively, yet are more mature in means of expression.

Imaginative play is an expressive medium for constructing and deconstructing, for inventing new forms of movement, and improvising and acting out imaginative possibilities. Using open-ended materials, we explore and imagine new patterns or designs with fabric, cardboard, paints, blocks, and other resources that become tools for liberating the play spirit. When we free ourselves from more restricted forms of expression, we generate optimism and origination.

Life itself becomes the unfolding play of consciousness. We engage in pretend play and become various actors, adventurers, directors, builders, and stage managers, freely moving in and out of playing various parts in the show life that we create together. Children organize, act, and make real within a pretend world. During moments of imaginative play, they make believe and alter and represent ideas about reality in original and unexpected ways. To understand a group of children, it helps to think of them as a traveling troupe of medieval players, who freely act out and respond to one another as though in a live theater. Transforming themselves through improvisation, they imagine and perform as artists, engineers, and poets, building, creating, and re-creating new worlds to explore in the moment of imaginative play (Sutton-Smith, 2001).

Sutton-Smith shares a view that within the state of play, similar to the experience of art, the player is drawn into the play, taken over, and held spellbound by the intense qualities of the play. Play is independent of the player's consciousness, so that the game plays the player and the person is changed by the experience of play expressed through the player (Sutton-Smith, 2001).

The game is what holds the player in the spell, draws him into play, and keeps him there. Much of the pleasure of playing lies in the fact that the game plays you—that your reactions are often more reflexive or involuntary than voluntary, that the game takes you out of yourself. It frees you from yourself by binding you to another (Sutton-Smith, 2001).

Play as Self in Pursuit of Peak Experience. The rhetoric of self interprets play as a subjective state of being, a mental view of the world, and one's own action that reveal a higher functioning state of being. Rather than being ordinary or mundane, play is a spiritual experience, the optimal flow, a way to connect with inner power and attaining higher consciousness. Play is intrinsically motivated, an intentional action that generates self-knowledge, acting with purpose, out of which comes self-actualized meaning and deeper understanding, a higher belief, wisdom, knowing one's self (Sutton-Smith, 2001).

During solitary play, one is projecting a future with optimism and experiencing the thrill derived from exploring possibilities. The important distinction is that there is an intrinsic relationship between self-discovery and play, not in terms of extrinsic issues about progress, power, or status. During play, there is a sense of playing with boundaries rather than being restricted by imposing rules that limit freedom. Through play, we access and discover the power to create harmony and order. There might be a sense of flow, of heightened awareness and self-discovery, as one merges consciousness with focused action. Self-discovery implies not only that we make the discoveries ourselves, but that we also discover the essential self.

Play as Adaptive Variability

Sutton-Smith presents his view that variability is the key to play and potential adaptation, whether as a child or adult. First is the idea that play serves to *actualize* what may be only potential brain or behavioral possibilities. In this scenario there is an awakening process resulting directly from play activity. Second is the likelihood that earlier actualization of neonatal development, such as unrealistic optimism, egocentricity, and reactivity, may fade in time, yet still remain *encapsulated* as possible expressions at any subsequent age. Thus, they may be qualities we draw upon later in life that were initially actualized as young children. Third is that play serves as an example of how we become an alternative expression of cultural variability through such play forms as music, dance, song, and the other arts, whether as professionals in these fields or leisure practitioners of the various options that help us to survive and sustain the human condition through art making. A fourth practical consideration is that there may be a transfer of play skills to our everyday skills existence which Sutton-Smith terms adaptive potentiation, making real and applying the skills developed during play. The fifth hypothetical formulation encapsulates each of the preceding four possibilities into a model of the exigent processes of adaptation that uses the virtual domain of play to learn ways of addressing and resolving conflict and uncertainties. The sixth speculation is that play's variability serves as a positive reinforcement mechanism for adaptive variability intended to promote and maintain resilience and flexibility, and insure our survival in the real world (Sutton-Smith, 2001).

CONCLUSION

Sutton-Smith concluded with "variability is the key to play, and that structurally play is characterized by quirkiness, redundancy, and flexibility" (Sutton-Smith, 2001, p. 229). It's not surprising that children enjoy play so much, given the characteristics of variability Sutton-Smith attributes to play. All of us are influenced to varying degrees by feelings and thoughts that generate anxiety and exert control over our behavior. At times the overwhelming challenges we face dominate and threaten our emotional existence. The variability of play serves as an antidote to despair, activating the potential of neural pathways and positive responses that relieve oppressive emotional forces and help in the struggle for survival.

REFERENCES

Brown, F., & Patte, M. (2012). From the streets of Wellington to the Ivy League: Reflecting on a lifetime of play—An interview with Brian Sutton-Smith. *International Journal of Play.* Vol.1:1. Taylor Francis.

Sutton-Smith, B. (2008). Play theory: A personal journey and new thoughts. *American Journal of Play, Summer*, The Strong National Museum of Play.

Sutton-Smith, B. (2007). *Play as the survival source of optimism and origination (The Double O).* A paper presented at the Florida Association for the Education of Young Children, (previously Early Childhood Association of Florida) Professional Development Day).

Sutton-Smith, B. (2001). *Ambiguity of play*. Harvard University Press.

12

Vivian Paley

1929–2019

Debora Wisneski

Vivian Paley.

> *If fantasy play provides the nourishing habitat for the growth of cognitive, narrative, and social connectivity in young children, then it is surely the staging area for our common enterprise: an early school experience that best represents the natural development of young children.* (Paley, 2004, p. 8)

Vivian Gussin Paley, a renowned American kindergarten teacher and author, is an inspiration and trusted guide for early childhood educators who endeavor to create inclusive and engaging early childhood classrooms that center learning on children's play. Through the process of close observation and analysis of children's interactions during play, as well as deep self-reflection, Paley developed an approach to teaching that put children's dignity and play at the heart of the curriculum and wrote thirteen books that describe her methods. Paley earned a PhB from the University of Chicago in 1947 and then taught school, first in New Orleans, and later in Great Neck, New York. Altogether, she taught preschool and kindergarten for 37 years with most of her time at the University of Chicago Laboratory School (Cooper, 2007).

EMPHASIS ON CLASSROOM PLAY

During her teaching career, Vivian Paley published books about children's play in the school setting that reflect her own learning about child development. The books portray how her thinking evolved as she became dissatisfied with traditional schooling methods that rely on worksheets and direct teaching. Paley recognized that the children were not engaged or learning, so she created a new system that utilizes classroom play and conversations.

Paley's books feature her musings that articulate insights into the ways that children express themselves during play. She recorded their conversations and transcribed the stories that they dictated to her. Next, Paley reviewed the artifacts, reflected on their meaning to her and to the children, and composed the texts that became popular books with educators, parents, and story lovers (Cooper, 2009).

Mentoring through Writing

Through this process of creating her books, Paley addressed a wide range of issues that arise in early childhood settings. Topics include understanding child development and thinking (such as in *Wally's Stories*, 1981, *Boys and Girls: Superheroes in the Doll Center*, 1984, and *Mollie is Three*, 1988), race and identity (in *White Teacher*, 1979, *Kwanzaa and Me*, 1995, and *The Girl with the Brown Crayon*, 1998), social inclusion and community (*The Boy*

Who Would be a Helicopter, 1990, *You Can't Say, You Can't Play*, 1993, and *The Kindness of Children*, 1999), and the ultimate treatise for play advocacy in early childhood school settings in *A Child's Work: The Importance of Fantasy Play* (2004). A brief sample of the play stories, conversations, and reflections can be seen here from *The Boy Who Would Be a Helicopter* (1990):

This is Katie's story:

> Once upon a time there was two little girls and a mommy and a daddy sleeped all together all in the same bed. And then they thinked of a monster with black ears and they put their capes on and creeped downstairs. And then we saw the monster inside our room.

"Creeped downstairs" comes from Ira. Every year certain phrases are planted and take root, the shoots continually coming up in stories and in play. Remember Joseph's alligator who creeped downstairs? The use of a communal symbol is as tangible a demonstration of socialization as the agreement to share blocks and dolls (p. 40).

In this excerpt, Paley shows how collecting children's stories and discussions allowed her to see the pattern of the children using the words "creeped downstairs" and understand how children used that language in their stories to connect with others socially. This is the style of Paley's writing, which reads like novels and allows the reader to enter the imaginary and lived worlds of the children and to enter into the researcher and philosopher mind of an exceptional teacher. While Paley rarely mentioned or cited developmental or play theorists in her texts, her commentaries and musings illuminated the foundational guiding theories of early childhood education and made them her own.

Recognition

Based on her extensive collection of children's play stories in school, Paley received many honors in her lifetime, such as the

- 1987 Erikson Institute Award for Service to Children,
- American Book Award from the Before Columbus Foundation for Lifetime Achievement in 1998,
- John Dewey Society's Outstanding Achievement Award in 2000, and
- Outstanding Educator of the Language Arts by the National Council of the Teachers of English in 2004.

Vivian Paley is best known for receiving the 1989 MacArthur Genius Fellowship Award. Her contributions to the understanding of play in the early years can be summarized in the areas of the play as curriculum through the storytelling/storyacting approach, the teacher role in play, and play as a form of community building.

Play as Curriculum through the Storytelling/StoryActing Approach

In an interview, Paley shared her perspective:

> Think dramatically. Get in the habit of thinking of yourself and the children as partners in an acting company. Once we learn to imagine ourselves as characters in a story, a particular set of events expands in all directions. We find ourselves being kinder and more respectful to one another because our options have grown in intimacy, humor, and literary flavor. (Dombrink-Green, 2011, p. 93)

While Paley advocated for play in many forms, pretend or imaginary play captured her own imagination and became her passion. Hence, many of her books include the different forms of stories acted out and discussed, particularly fairy tales, children's literature stories, and the stories the children told or acted out as they played. Eventually, Paley (1990) created a process of storytelling and storyacting as explained in *The Boy Who Would Be a Helicopter*.

In this process the children would dictate their stories to Paley and she would write them down throughout the kindergarten day. In the process of writing down the stories, Paley would often ask questions for clarification so that she honored the meaning and intent of the story. Later, the class as a whole group would come together and sit in a square marked off by tape on the floor. The open space in the center was considered the stage. Paley (1990) would then select actors from the group of children to be the actors for the characters of the "play." The child-author of the story could choose to participate as an actor or not.

Next, Paley (1990) would slowly read the dictated story to the children and the chosen actors who now were standing in the center of the "stage" would act out the story as told. After the story was read and acted out, the class of children could discuss their thoughts and feelings about the story. The process transformed Paley's view of teaching. She stated, "Once I began to view the children as storytellers and playwrights, the potential of fantasy as a learning tool overwhelmed my conventional expectations for the classroom" (p.19).

Paley began to appreciate the intricate interactions of the children between the telling of the story, the listening of the story, the acting out of the story, the consideration and comparisons of the story and the children's discussions of their interpretations of the story. Each of these aspects of the process supported the children's learning. Play alone, story alone, and discussion alone were not enough to engage the children and to understand them.

Paley (1990) described the children's stories and their play as the basis of the early childhood classroom curriculum. These "dramatic impulses of play" (p. 30) helped children to organize complex ideas. Many researchers in the field of early childhood education and development have explored this notion of storytelling/storyacting as a learning tool by examining the ways in which children learn through this process. Mostly, the identified learning outcomes in these studies include early literacy skills, such as narrative creation, oral language and vocabulary development, and listening. However, there is emerging research interest that views early learning in much broader terms beyond school standards or subject areas, and searches for understanding how children learn about democratic and community practices.

The Teacher's Role in Play

Vivian Paley articulated the power of teachers to facilitate narratives when she said, "I have discovered something important about children. Anything that happens during their play or storytelling makes for captivating conversation as long as I am sincere" (Paley, 1990, p. 32).

While there is professional consensus within the field of early childhood education that learning through play is the optimal way for children to learn, there is often debate in what the teacher's role should be during the children's play. Paley's play stories reveal a very deliberate way for teachers to engage with children that balances the child's voice and choices with a teacher's guidance. She emphasized the role of observation along with documentation, intense listening to children's stories and explanations of their play, dialogue with sincere questioning, and thoughtful reflection on the content of the play process (Cooper, 2009).

Paley's keen observation skills and her ability to engage in intense listening is evident in the ways she recounts play episodes. The details of play that accompany the dictation of their stories and transcripts of their conversations are at the heart of understanding children and play. Without this depth and detail of documentation, making meaning of the play could be difficult and muddled. However, with the details captured, the reader and the teacher can see into the world of the child's play. Currently, in an American educational context that is heavily focused on data-driven decision making as part of the teaching process, Paley's books highlight that the most critical data are the play stories in the classroom (Cooper, 2009).

As mentioned, Paley (1990) also engaged in deep dialogue and questioning of the children about their play stories. This approach was developed based on the children's own questioning of each other. Paley stated,

> They question one another continually in play and I simply do as they do. I have, in fact, learned from them about question asking. They seldom, for instance, ask a question of another child if they already know the answer." (p. 23) Hence, Paley's questioning of the children was not with the intent to "test" the children on their knowledge, but was based in a sincere desire to understand the child and the play. Paley also discovered that play often interrupted with questions by the children was a form of the "social art of language." (Paley, 1990, p. 23)

Paley believed that teachers should reflect on the meaning of play stories. Hence, as seen in her texts, no play episode was shared without a discussion and commentary on how Paley made sense of play. She also reflected with others, extending the play dialogue to other adults—teachers, parents, grown-up former students from her classes—to help gain a better understanding of the play (Cooper, 2009).

Play as a Form of Community Building

According to Paley, children's play in the context of school was different than the free play in their own home. School provided a context of the larger society which a child enters. The classroom was a space in which all children belong.

> The stories are mainly about love and friendship, no matter if the wolf is howling or the kittens are meowing. One role is as good as another, so long as you can be inside the story and become necessary to the group. (Paley, 2010, p. 90)

Hence, many of Paley's reflections and books focused on how all children can be included in play. She noticed two things: 1) when children tell and play out their stories, they become connected socially and begin to build a culture of inclusion and belonging that affects other activities through the school day, and 2) in spite of the cohesive community that is in the process of building through play, some children are often left out (Paley, 2010).

Based on Paley's moral vision of play and school, the burden of exclusion should not fall on the children that are excluded. Rather, the responsibility lies on the group as a whole to consider how the excluded can find a place in the play and stories. Paley summarizes her beliefs in *White Teacher* (1979):

> Those of us who have been outsiders understand the need to be seen exactly as we are and to be accepted and valued. Our safety lies in schools and societies in

which faces with many shapes and colors can feel an equal sense of belonging. Our children must grow up knowing and liking those who look and speak in different ways, or they will live as strangers in a hostile land. (p. 139)

Many of Paley's books show how different children are included in play, but Paley directly addresses the problem of exclusion in play in the text *You Can't Say, You Can't Play*. She recognized that, if not interrupted, children grow up thinking it is okay for those with more power to reject others. So, she introduced a new class rule for her kindergartners, "You can't say, you can't play." The process of the children's struggle with the new rule of inclusion in play reveals the strong desire for some children to control play and others, and yet slowly also shows how the children learn to treat each other more kindly.

Paley's Continued Influence on Play in Early Childhood Education

Based on the extensive documentation of the play and stories of her early childhood classrooms and her abundant professional conference presentations during her career, Paley laid the foundation for others to explore the power of play and stories in early childhood settings. She offered personal guidance to those who inquired about her work with children and also often helped connect professionals across the world with each other to encourage the exchange of ideas. In essence, she was encouraging the dialogue and questioning to continue beyond her classroom play stories.

While research continues to grow around storytelling/storyacting and other aspects of Paley's play with young children, interested readers might enjoy the work of two authors that elaborated on the theme; Gillian McNamee, who wrote *The High-Performing Preschool* (2015) and Patricia Cooper, who wrote *When Stories Come to School* (1993, 2007) and *The Classrooms All Young Children Need* (2009).

As more early childhood teachers begin to incorporate storytelling/storyacting in their daily school curriculum, concerted efforts to support Paley's approach to play can be seen in the Boston Public Schools in the United States. In 2012–2013, with the leadership of Ben Mardel and Jason Sachs, the Boston public schools began a pilot program in fifty classrooms using the storytelling/storyacting approach. Now this approach is part of the preschool and kindergarten curriculum of all Boston public schools called Boston Listens. In collaboration with Paley in 2002, Trish Lee began training teachers in the United Kingdom to develop the storytelling/storyacting technique called Helicopter Stories, which eventually became part of a program in a comprehensive charity group called Make Believe Arts (McNamee, 2015).

Gillian McNamee (2005) captured Paley's contribution to play in early childhood as the following:

> Paley found that listening to children, giving them the experience of being heard, and valuing their point of view fundamentally changed her. She learned that in order to teach, to be heard, she had to listen. Because she cared so deeply about what children were thinking and how their thinking developed, she invited, cultivated, and encouraged the children's play. The more she did, the more benefits she reaped; the more articulate, creative and expressive the children became. Her collected works now show how her methodology of teaching through fostering pretend play can be repeated year after year with groups of children from diverse backgrounds, and lead to the same results—highly educated children. (p. 278)

CONCLUSION

Not only has Paley shown us how young children can become highly educated through play, she has also demonstrated how we all can live as kinder and wiser members of society through play, as well. In *Wally's Stories* (1981), Paley noted, "I do not ask the children to stop thinking about play" (p. 223). Due to her dedication to children's play, many educators, researchers, and parents will also not stop thinking about play.

REFERENCES

Cooper, P. M. (1993, 2007). *When stories come to school: Telling, writing & performing stories in the early childhood classroom*. Teachers and Writers Collaborative.

Cooper, P. M. (2009). *The classrooms all young children need: Lessons in teaching from Vivian Paley*. The University of Chicago Press.

Dombrink-Green, M. (2011). A conversation with Vivian Gussin Paley. *YC Young Children, 66*, 5, 90.

McNamee, G.D. (2005) "The one who gathers children": The work of Vivian Gussin Paley and current debates about how we educate young children, *Journal of Early Childhood Teacher Education*, 25:3, 275-296, DOI: 10.1080/1090102050250311

McNamee, G. D. (2015). *The high performing preschool: Story acting in head start classrooms*. University of Chicago Press.

Paley, V. G. (1979). *White teacher*. Harvard University Press.

Paley, V. G. (1981). *Wally's stories*. Harvard University Press.

Paley, V. G. (1984). *Boys and girls: Superheroes in the doll corner*. University of Chicago Press.

Paley, V. G. (1988) *Mollie is three: Growing up in school*. University of Chicago Press.

Paley, V. G. (1990). *The boy who would be a helicopter*. Harvard University Press.
Paley, V. G. (1998). *The girl with the brown crayon*. Harvard University Press.
Paley, V. G. (1995). *Kwanzaa and me: A teacher's story*. Harvard University Press.
Paley, V. G. (1993). *You can't say, you can't play*. Harvard University Press.
Paley, V. G. (1999). *The kindness of children*. Harvard University Press.
Paley, V. G. (2004). *A child's work: The importance of fantasy play*. University of Chicago Press.
Paley, V. G. (2010). *The boy on the beach: Building community through play*. University of Chicago Press.

13

Joe L. Frost

1933–2020

John Sutterby

Joe L. Frost.

> *We've complicated something so essentially innocent and straightforward—kids just need a safe setting where they can become strong and resilient and develop into thinkers, builders, creators, and explorers.* (Frost & Sutterby, 2017)

Joe L. Frost was born into a community in the Ouachita Mountains of Western Arkansas. He recalls fondly his time playing before school, during extended lunch breaks and after school. These breaks involved being engaged with nature as he roamed the mountains and forests. Some of the games he played with his friends might not be so popular today. Hot Pants, for example, was a game that involved lighting a piece of paper in someone's back pocket and seeing how far that person could run before having to put out the fire. Obviously, most of his early play experiences had very little adult supervision (American Journal of Play, 2008; Frost, 2010).

The community he lived in at the time was extremely impoverished. Many children went to school hungry, and some even turned to eating clay to fill their empty stomachs. Perhaps Frost's emphasis on advocacy for children came out of this childhood experience. After a stint building military aircraft as a mechanic, Frost returned to Arkansas to complete his PhD in 1965. He eventually ended up at the University of Texas at Austin in 1966 where he held a faculty position until his retirement in 2000. Upon his retirement, he was awarded the Parker Centennial Professor Emeritus Professorship (Moore, 2017; Link, 2017).

ADVOCATE FOR CHILDREN

An overarching theme for all of Dr. Frost's work was the focus on advocacy for children. His earliest works examined the life experiences of children in poverty. At the time, "disadvantaged" was in vogue as "a euphemism for the poor" (Frost & Hawkes, 1970, p. 1). Since then we have gone through numerous other euphemisms for the poor. As an advocate for children, Frost, from the beginning, reflected on how early experiences, especially negative ones like disease or malnutrition, can have negative consequences later in life (Frost & Payne, 1970). Frost built his career on advocacy for early childhood education, opportunities for children to engage with nature, and opportunities for them to play in safe places.

Play Deprivation and Child Development

Joe L. Frost began his professorship at the University of Texas at Austin in 1966, the same year that Charles Whitman barricaded himself in the University of Texas Tower with a cache of weapons. Whitman opened fire on the students and faculty, killing 16 people and wounding over 30 others until he himself was killed by an Austin police officer. This shocking event eventually led to an investigation into the life of Whitman by Stuart Brown to find what might have been the root cause of this terrible tragedy. Dr. Brown eventually concluded that Whitman had been severely abused as a child with few opportunities to play. Further study found that lack of play correlated with negative outcomes for children into adulthood (Campos & Moore, 2017).

As he learned about play deprivation and neurological development, Frost shifted his focus to advocating for child play. Research on children who have had little opportunity for play and interactions with others indicates that substantial brain damage can occur. In many cases, strong interactions and opportunities to engage in play have lessened some of the consequences of this deprivation (Frost, Wortham, & Reifel, 2012).

Play deprivation also has consequences for children's healthy social, physical, and emotional development. Frost's observations of rough and tumble play show how that type of play can lead to positive social outcomes (Brown, 2009). He explored the importance of play and healthy physical development through decades of research at the Redeemer Lutheran School in Austin, Texas. His research included different aspects of children's physical development such as brachiation, rhythm and coordination, and how they are enhanced through play (Frost, Brown, Sutterby, & Thornton, 2004).

Play is an important factor in keeping children physically fit and in reducing the risk of obesity (Frost & Sutterby, 2002). Play and its relationship to emotional development is also well documented. Frost discusses how play's therapeutic properties can help children survive natural disasters. Opportunities to play and create meaningful works, often with guidance from adults, can help children cope with their situation (Frost, 2005).

Frost and Brown have presented many times together on the topic of the importance of play for healthy children's development and how play deprivation can negatively impact children. More recently their focus turned to the negative impacts on children's play such as electronics, increased stress due to school testing, and the elimination of recess in many places. They view this form of play deprivation in this case as more a factor of culture rather than a situation imposed as a deliberate form of abuse (Brown, 2017; Frost, 2010).

Playground Design

Frost also focused on playground design and the historical development of playgrounds. In addition to writing about design, he designed the overall environments and participated in numerous playground building projects.

Frost's interest in design began with playground projects at the Redeemer Lutheran School playground in 1973, which coincided with the beginning of the Community Playground Movement (Sutterby, 2017; Frost & Sutterby 2017).

The playground movement promoted the use of natural and cast-off materials to make more interesting and unique playgrounds. Old cars and boats, tires and ropes were used as inexpensive materials to create these playgrounds. The Playground Checklist developed by Frost has an entry for "a purchased or built vehicle, airplane, boat or car that has been made safe" (Frost et al., 2004, p. 227). Some of the influence was derived from European Adventure playgrounds that were much more interactive and organic than traditional United States playgrounds that typically contained heavy fixed equipment like slides and climbers (Frost, 1978).

As Frost began to develop courses in play and play environments, he began to attract graduate and doctoral students interested in play and playgrounds. He taught influential designers such as James Jolley, Jim Dempsey, Eric Strickland, and others in the UT Austin doctoral program. Their innovative designs changed how playgrounds were made (Frost, 1991). Many of these research projects took place at the Redeemer Lutheran School, which was an environment that welcomed innovation of their playgrounds over time and continues to celebrate a culture of play as part of their whole child curriculum (Frost et al., 2004).

Frost also has been influential in textbook publications on outdoor environments. His series of textbooks were some of the first academic sources examining outdoor play environments. Starting with his work with Barry Klein (Frost & Klein, 1979), Frost has documented innovative designs and designers as well as principals of playground environment development that serve to provide playground developers with a foundation based on the latest research in play and child development (Frost, 1991; Frost et al., 2004; Frost, Wortham, & Reifel, 2012).

In addition to participating in playground building, Frost designed play spaces at hospitals, parks, and even the San Antonio Zoo. These projects serve as a model for what playgrounds can truly be. Unfortunately, according to Frost, various factors such as new government regulations, the Americans with Disabilities Act, parental fear of risk, and manufacturers' concern for litigation have led to cookie cutter playgrounds that offer little challenge to children and thus less interest in playing in these play spaces (American Journal of Play, 2008). As an antidote to the cookie cutter playground, Frost pursued natural play spaces because forests, streams, and hills provide unique affordances for children's play that cannot be matched by manufactured equipment (Frost, 2010).

Playground Safety

Ensuring playground safety involves a delicate balancing act between putting children at risk of serious injury and making environments so uninteresting that children find other ways to entertain themselves. As an advocate for children's welfare, Joe Frost has been at the forefront of academics discussing safety and playgrounds. He documented how safety standards evolved over time. Historically, since safety was not a major concern on early playgrounds, surfaces were hard and equipment was built to great heights. Although there were some concerns raised about hard surfacing like asphalt on playgrounds at schools, it was still seen as preferable to the dust and mud that it replaced (Frost & Henniger, 1979; Frost, 1985; Frost, Wortham, and Reifel, 2012).

It was not until the late 1960s that safety standards were officially considered for playgrounds. Researchers began to look into the risks of faulty equipment and falling onto hard surfaces. Injury data that was collected to identify common injuries using the National Electronic Injury Survey System (NEISS) led to the development of safety standards by the Consumer Product Safety Commission (CPSC). Playground equipment designers consult these standards to develop their equipment. As a result, resilient surfacing, reduced fall heights, smooth equipment, and the removal of heavy animal swings have become standard practice for playgrounds based on these standards (Frost, 1985).

Unfortunately, the major driving force for playground safety over time has been litigation. Joe Frost reluctantly got involved in litigation as an expert witness related to child development, play, and playground design. He and Theodora Sweeney served as expert witnesses for more than 200 lawsuits based on playground injuries and deaths. From their experience, they determined that falls to hard surfaces were the major cause of injuries on playgrounds. They also identified excessive heights on equipment as a major cause of injuries and violations of the CPSC guidelines were identified in more than half of these cases. Most of the cases they participated in were settled out of court (Frost & Sweeney, 1996).

Currently, litigation is still a major factor in playground design. Playground safety standards continue to evolve and parents continue to try to create a risk-free environment for their children. To ameliorate the risk factor, Frost advocated for playground supervision by trained play leaders. Although common in European adventure playgrounds, the play leader concept has not yet been taken seriously by budget minded policy makers in the United States. (Frost, Wortham & Reifel, 2012).

Play and Nature

Always hopeful, Dr. Frost became involved in the Back to Nature Movement, which was greatly popularized by the work of Richard Louv (2005). Reflecting on his childhood, Frost has always attributed his emotional and spiritual health to his early opportunities to play in the outdoors in the forests and mountains. He has frequently voiced his concern that children today do not have those same opportunities due to factors such as an emphasis on electronic entertainment and parental fear of the outdoors. He draws many of his beliefs about the importance of play and nature from the work of Friedrich Froebel and his nature-based curriculum in the kindergarten (Frost, 2008).

Joe Frost championed the development of nature play in the gardens at the Redeemer Lutheran School. Additionally, the water retention pond became an area where children could feel close to nature as they wandered through the tall reeds in the shade of cypress trees. This space seemed magical to the children and was a place where they could engage all of their senses. It can serve as a model for other schools looking to enhance children's access to nature (Frost, Keyburn & Sutterby, 2010).

Looking nationally, Frost focused on the many organizations which are working to reacquaint children with nature. He examined everything from the School Garden Movement to the Organized Camping Movement. Working mostly independently, these organizations are reflective of the rising concern about children's early experiences in the outdoors. Collectively, they are part of what Frost calls the Contemporary Child-Saving Movement. This gives rise to hope that children's lives and welfare will continue to improve (Frost, 2010).

CONCLUSION

Joe Frost was a leader in the world of play, who worked for the benefit and welfare of young children. His beliefs, which were rooted in his deep faith in humanity, shaped his advocacy for children's opportunities to play in safe and engaging environments that would engage their minds and spirits. The education community and the play community were especially fortunate to have Joe Frost as an advocate for play.

REFERENCES

Brown, S. (2009). *Play: How it shapes the brain, opens the imagination and invigorates the soul.* Avery.

Brown, S. (2017). Play deprivation. In M. Moore & C. Sabo-Risley (Eds.) *Play in American Life* (pp. 27–34). Archway Publishing.

Campos, D., & Moore, M. (2017). The lasting effects of the UT Austin Tower Massacre. In M. Moore & C. Sabo-Risley (Eds.) *Play in American Life* (pp. 35–46). Archway Publishing.

Frost, J. (1978). The American playground movement. *Childhood Education 54*, 4, 176–182.

Frost, J. (1985). The history of playground safety in American. *Children's Environments Quarterly, 2,* 4, 13–23.

Frost, J. (1991). *Play and playscapes.* Delmar.

Frost, J. (2005). Lessons from disasters: Play, work and the creative arts. *Childhood Education, 82,* 1, 2–8.

Frost, J. (2008). What's wrong with America's playgrounds and how to fix them. *American Journal of Play, 1,* 2, 139–156.

Frost, J. (2010). *A history of children's play and play environments.* Routledge.

Frost, J., Brown, P., Sutterby, J., & Thornton, C. (2004). *The developmental benefits of playgrounds.* Association for Childhood Education International.

Frost, J., & Hawkes, G. (1970). *The disadvantaged child: Issues and innovations.* Houghton Mifflin Company.

Frost, J., & Henniger, M. (1979). Making playgrounds safe for children and children safe for playgrounds. *Young Children 34,* 5, 23–30.

Frost, J., Keyburn, D., & Sutterby, J. (2010). Notes from the land down under: Transforming a sterile urban schoolyard into a nature wonderland. In J. Hoot & J. Szente (Eds.) *The earth is our home: Children caring for the environment*, pp. 131–147. Association for Childhood Education International.

Frost, J., & Klein, B. (1979). *Play and playgrounds.* Allyn and Bacon.

Frost, J., & Payne, B. (1970). Hunger in America: Scope and sequence. In J. Frost & G. Hawkes (Eds.) *The disadvantaged child: Issues and innovations*, pp. 70–83. Houghton Mifflin Company.

Frost, J., & Sutterby, J. (2002). Making playgrounds fit for children and children fit on playgrounds. *Young Children, 57,* 3, 36–41.

Frost, J., & Sutterby, J. (2017). Outdoor play is essential to whole child development. *Young Children, 72,* 3, 82–85.

Frost, J., & Sweeney, T. (1996). *Cause and prevention of playground injuries and litigation: Case studies.* Association for Childhood Education International.

Frost, J., Wortham, S., & Reifel, S. (2012). *Play and child development* (4th ed). Pearson.

Link, J. (2017). Designer profile: Joe Frost: The contemporary father of play advocacy. On line at https://goric.com/designer-profile-joe-frost-contemporary-father-play-advocacy/

Louv, R. (2005). *The last child in the woods: Saving our children from nature deficit disorder.* Algonquin Books.

Moore, M. (2017). The life and work of Joe L. Frost: An introduction. In M. Moore & C. Sabo-Risley (Eds.) *Play in American Life* (pp. x–xii). Archway Publishing.

Sutterby, J. (2017). From the park to the playground: Building for democracy. In M. Moore & C. Sabo-Risley (Eds.) *Play in American Life* (pp. 155–165). Archway Publishing.

14

Louise Derman-Sparks

1940–

Kenya Wolff

Louise Derman-Sparks.

Play is central to the anti-bias curriculum.

Throughout her career as an educator and social activist, Louise Derman-Sparks has been an enthusiastic proponent of play. In a 2016 publication (Derman-Sparks & Moore, 2016), she states that "richly providing for children's active learning, nurturing dramatic play, and offering a balance of child- and teacher-directed activities and paying attention to the inseparable connection between social-emotional and cognitive development" was a crucial part of the success she experienced in her first years of teaching at Ypsilanti Perry Preschool (p. 5). As one of the original teachers at the preschool, Louise Derman-Sparks initiated anti-bias practices and implemented lessons to foster equity as part of her mission to promote peace education.

AGENT OF CHANGE

After receiving recognition for her early work, Derman-Sparks was inspired to serve as an agent of change on a grander scale. Widely acclaimed for her efforts to challenge prejudice, she is an author whose numerous books on anti-bias education have had a profound influence on educators, social activists, and policy makers around the world. In addition to her experience in preschool, Derman-Sparks served on the Governing Board for the National Association for the Education of Young Children (1998 to 2001) and taught at Pacific Oaks College for 33 years. In her original groundbreaking publication, *Anti-Bias Curriculum: Tools for Empowering Young Children*, she shared the story of the ABC Taskforce (Derman-Sparks, 1989) It portrays the work of twelve early childhood educators who collaborated to create an anti-bias curriculum.

For the next twenty years, the anti-bias model was adopted by teacher preparation programs and educators alike, filling an essential need to prepare children for pluralistic societies. The book provided developmentally appropriate teaching methods that sought to counter the biases (and -isms) that plague society. Twenty-one years later, Derman-Sparks and Olsen Edwards expanded the conceptualization of diversity beyond race, gender, ethnicity, culture, and religion to include socio-economic class, family structures, language, immigrant families, and sexual orientation in an updated version of the book, *Anti-Bias Education for Young Children and Ourselves* (Derman-Sparks & Edwards, 2010).

Play in the Anti-Bias Curriculum

In all of her work, Derman-Sparks acknowledges the power of play and advocates for integrating play-based activities into the daily routine. An emphasis on play is deeply embedded within anti-bias curriculum, which is grounded in the philosophy that if educators don't intentionally and actively counter the racism, sexism, and other "isms" that presently exist in our communities, then children will learn these messages by default (Derman-Sparks, 1989).

The books pertaining to anti-bias curriculum and instruction feature both child- and teacher-initiated activities. Built on constructivist principles, they are profoundly influenced by the principles of developmentally appropriate practice (DAP). Practitioners of DAP believe that children act out cultural norms during play such as gender roles, cultural values, and power dynamics. Children also communicate their awareness about differences when they play by indicating preferences in regard to gender, race, and ability, as demonstrated by their choice of playmates and toy selections (Derman-Sparks,1989; Derman-Sparks & Phillips,1997; Derman-Sparks & Ramsey, 2006; Derman-Sparks & Edwards, 2010).

Teachers can discern teachable moments for addressing bias by carefully observing play. For example, in the chapter on toddlers, Derman-Sparks (1989) warns,

> They must do their own learning, as they interact with the physical world and each other. Formal lessons taught by adults just don't work! Consequently, planning primarily consists of all aspects of the classroom environment. Children's play, comments, and questions then become the basis for interactions between child and teacher that address anti-bias issues. (p. 21)

Gender and Play

> *How do you know if you are a girl or a boy? the teacher asks a group of preschoolers. Everyone has an idea. Boys wear pants . . . girls have long hair . . . boys play with trucks, girls like to sit.* (Derman-Sparks & Edwards, 2010, p. 90)
>
> *A four-year-old boy, wanting to take over the wheel of a pretend bus, tells the child already there, "Girls can't be bus drivers."* (Derman-Sparks, 1989, p. ix)

Gender is the first identity characteristic that most children notice. Two-year-old children begin to observe gender differences and to describe themselves as a boy or a girl, even if they don't understand what that means. By the age of three, children are able to articulate the roles, activities, toys, and behaviors that are stereotyped as either masculine or feminine. For example, *boys don't cook* or *girls play with dolls*. By age four, children are fairly strict in their beliefs about gender roles and by age five they've adopted wholeheartedly their family's expectations and the greater societal beliefs surrounding gender identity (Derman-Sparks, 1989).

While young children may notice gender early, many preschoolers don't understand what actually makes them a girl or a boy. Many look to external aspects, like long hair, or to behavioral aspects, like *girls like dolls*, rather than to gender anatomy. Young children also have a difficult time understanding gender consistency, believing that they can switch genders. Derman-Sparks and Edwards (2010) shared the following passage,

> Caitlyn puts on a hard hat and goes to play at the woodworking table. "Look at me, she announces. Now I am a boy. Later I will be a girl again." (p. 91)

It is important for educators to help children understand gender while also challenging the stereotypes that exist in our dominant culture. This can be difficult when it comes to working with families. One concern that parents may express is the fear that sexual orientation is connected to the types of play a child engages in during recess. For example, "A parent asks the teacher to keep his child out of the dramatic play area because playing there undermines cultural values about the role of men" (Derman-Sparks, LeeKeenan, & Nimmo, 2015, p. 44). Teachers must understand and help parents to understand that there is no type of play that can lead to homosexuality just as there is no type of play that can undo homosexuality.

The anti-bias approach to gender and play within the classroom is to give children the freedom to select their toys, play activities, and pretend scenarios. The majority of toys marketed to girls are either dolls or cleaning or beauty products. The toys marketed toward boys are more action based. The marketing of toys based on these defined gender roles supports and perpetuates patriarchy which is the current social system in which males are perceived as dominant and females are expected to be subordinate (Derman-Sparks & Edwards, 2010).

In the dramatic play area, an anti-bias approach to guidance can have a powerful influence on behavior. Teachers are encouraged to supplement the housekeeping items with drills, hammers, tool belts, calculators, laptops, and cell phones to diminish stereotypes about play choices. If a teacher notices the girls avoiding the block center or boys refusing to do art, they can provide opportunities for children to expand their play so that they gain confidence in these areas. Teachers can explain that it is important for girls to learn to build with blocks too, and even create building challenges by offering theme days for building with blocks, one for *everybody*, another for *girls only* (Derman-Sparks & Edwards, 2010).

Gender and Sexualized Toys

In Derman-Sparks and Edward's (2010) chapter on "Learning about Gender Diversity and Fairness," in which they wrote a section about the "sexualization of childhood," they discussed the highly sexualized context children are exposed to in which marketers often use violence to market to boys and use sexualized images of girls to make toys and clothes more appealing.

The objectification of girls as sexual objects valued for their appearance and the stereotyping of boys as needing to be tough, can be challenged in the classroom. Teachers need to make sure they aren't perpetuating this by making statements that focus on girls' dress and appearance in the morning when they come in, or excusing boys' aggression by saying, *boys will be boys* or, after getting hurt, *toughen up,* or *boys don't cry*. Teachers can seek opportunities to refute and dispel gendered messages and encourage girls and boys to explore interests that may be off limits or discouraged because of their gender (Derman-Sparks & Edwards, 2010).

Concepts of ethnicity

> *You can't be a princess! Princesses have blonde hair! Announces a White three-year-old to an African American friend.* (Derman-Sparks & Edwards, 2010, p. 1)
>
> *If I'm Black and White, and Tiffany is Black and White, why is her skin darker.* (Derman-Sparks & Edwards, 2010, p. 77)
>
> *"I'm going to make my eyes straight and blue," four-year-old Cindy tells her teacher.*
>
> *"Why do you want to change your lovely eyes?" Danica, her teacher, wonders. "It's prettier" Cindy says.* (Derman-Sparks & Edwards, 2010, p. 83)

The concept of race is a social construct and not a scientific or biological scientific term. Within the United States, it has been used to categorize, subjugate, and oppress groups of people. Racial identity is also a key component of social identity, along with gender, religion, ability, culture, and home language. Children are bombarded by covert and overt messages about racial identity, and many of them, which are mistaken, misleading, or confusing, may lead children to internalize feelings of superiority and/or inferiority (Derman-Sparks & Edwards, 2010).

In play, this can surface in many ways. In the well-known Clark Doll Test, researchers found that, when given a choice, black preschool children opted to play with white dolls more often than the black ones. In the same study, children tended to use words like *pretty* and *good* when describing the white dolls and referred to the black dolls as *ugly* and *bad*.

Researchers theorized that the black preschoolers had internalized the bias surrounding them. White dominance can lead to the opposite—internalized racial superiority (Derman-Sparks & Phillips, 1997). This can be seen in the following play scenario: Two five-year-old white boys are playing in the sandbox. A Vietnamese boy asks to join them. "Nah, nah, you can't play with us, you Chinese," they chorus, pulling their eyes into a slant (Derman, 1989, p. 34).

Racial Identity

It is important for teachers to understand that "children's racial identity is shaped from the outside but constructed from the inside" (Derman-Sparks & Olesen, 2010, p. 83). Thus, educators can help children to develop positive self-affect about their own racial identity and learn to respect and appreciate the racial diversity of others. When implementing the anti-bias curriculum, educators must consider the following points about young children:

- Infants and toddlers show an awareness of skin color.
- Three-year-olds discuss their own and others' aspects of racial identity such as skin color, hair texture, and so on.
- Young children want explanations about why children look different from them and if they don't get them, they will make up their own (for example, my hair is white so it is cleaner than your hair that is brown). Preschoolers need help resisting harmful messages about their racial identity.
- Children who are biracial or multiracial and children who have been adopted will have additional questions and concerns about their own identity. (Derman-Sparks & Edwards, 2010)

Socio-Economic Status and Play

> *"I got more toys than you did. I got a new trike and Candy Land game and two new dolls and lots more! What did you get for your birthday?"*
>
> *"You can't play with us because you do not have the latest, expensive, well-advertised toy."* (Derman-Sparks & Edwards, 2010, p. 104)

Issues regarding economic status impact all children. It is important for teachers working with children from high-income families to understand the early signs of entitlement and superiority and to watch for signs from children from low-income families to look for signs that they are feeling less than equal. Often this comes out in play.

Derman-Sparks and Edwards (2010) share many effective ways that teachers can support equity in the play environment. For example, when talking about community helpers and placing items in the dramatic play area, educators should include a variety of employment options. Teachers should ask parents who work as cashiers, janitors, and construction workers to visit to help children feel proud of their family and foster the understanding that everyone contributes to the community. Children's nooks in the library need to show children living in a variety of circumstances, such as homes, apartments, and trailers. They should also show families using laundromats, riding the bus, and using other types of transportation. By including children from low-income backgrounds in the visual images and narrative, they can develop an understanding of different lifestyles (Derman-Sparks & Edwards, 2010).

Educators must also be sensitive to issues surrounding food. For children who have experienced hunger, it can be perplexing and insensitive to use food to create art or to play with in the sensory table. Adopt a policy that food is exclusively for eating. It is important to teach respect for the sanctity of food and avoid sending the message that food is something some people have so much of that they can use it for play (Derman-Sparks & Edwards, 2010).

Guidelines for Anti-Bias Practice

Teachers are encouraged to create anti-bias classroom environments, materials, and activities that are bias free. The first step is for teachers to examine their own implicit and explicit bias. Teacher attitudes about race and ethnicity can and do impact the classroom, because children pick up on subtle messages about who is important, who is included, and what is allowed to be said in the classroom. Allow students to ask questions about race and then answer as simply and honestly as you can in a straightforward manner (Derman-Sparks, 1989).

Materials also send a message about what is important. Choose books that portray multicultural themes and characters that counter stereotypes and celebrate cultural differences. Make sure that the "play" food in the dramatic play center represents diverse cultural options, and provide multicultural paints and crayons available in the art center. Additionally, invite community members from a variety of backgrounds to visit and interact with the class. Offer a variety of puppets, dolls, posters, and music that represent a spectrum of diversity and not just a token image of any particular group (Derman-Sparks & Edwards, 2010).

During children's play, teachers need to be vigilant in order to detect teasing or instances of exclusive behaviors. If an inappropriate social situation does occur, teachers must address the situation with sensitivity and, perhaps, approach it with one of the following strategies:

- Use puppets, storytelling, and books to help children develop empathy and respect in relationships.
- Encourage perspective taking by asking children, "how would you feel if this happened to you?" Help children to be assertive when they feel hurt and to learn to stand up for themselves and others (Derman-Sparks & Edwards, 2010).

Derman-Sparks was often asked in discussions with educators of young children, How should we teach about race and multiculturalism in all-white classrooms? Her response was to write a book with Patricia Ramsey: *What if all the kids are white? Anti-bias multicultural education with young children and families* (Derman-Sparks & Ramsey, 2006) that offers the following guidelines:

- Work to acquire identities built on their individual interests, talents, experiences and culture
- Understand that all people have a range of differences and similarities
- Respect and value attributes that are new to them
- Challenge the idea that everyone is like them and should be like them
- Learn empathy and conflict resolution
- Identify and counter stereotypes, prejudice and unfairness within the classroom and their communities
- Learn how to be an ally through hearing stories of whites who have fought for equity and social justice (Derman-Sparks & Ramsey, 2006)

CONCLUSION

Play is central to the anti-bias curriculum. Anti-bias philosophies can be incorporated into practice as evidenced by the materials selected for dramatic play, art, block center, writing, and library centers, as well as in thoughtful discussions. Teachers are facilitators for the children who are viewed as active learners, who are guided by their own interests and are constructing their own knowledge through play.

REFERENCES

Clark, K., & Clark, M. (1939). The development of consciousness of self and the emergence of racial identification in Negro preschool children. *Journal of Social Psychology*, *10*, 4, 591–599. doi:10.1080/00224545.1939.9713394.

Derman-Sparks, L. (1989). *Anti-Bias curriculum: Tools for empowering young children*. National Association for the Education of Young Children.

Derman-Sparks, L., & Phillips, C. B. (1997). *Teaching/learning anti-racism: A developmental approach*. Teachers College Press.

Derman-Sparks L., & Ramsey, P. G. (2006). *What if all the kids are white? Anti-bias multicultural education with young children and families*. Teachers College Press.

Derman-Sparks, L., & Edwards, J. (2010). *Anti-bias education for young children and ourselves*. National Association for the Education of Young Children.

Derman-Sparks, L., LeeKeenan, D., & Nimmo, J. (2015). Building anti-bias early childhood programs: The role of the leader. *Young Children, 70*, 2, 42–45.

Derman-Sparks, L., & Moore, E. K. (2016). Our proud heritage: Lessons for today the Ypsilanti Perry Preschool, Part I. *Young Children*, *71*, 4, 1–9.

15

Olivia Natividad Saracho

1942–

Edith Esparza and Matilde A. Sarmiento

Olivia Natividad Saracho.

Through play, young children become active learners.

Eldest daughters, who often serve as caretakers for their families, cultivate watchful eyes as they anticipate the needs of younger siblings. Olivia Saracho acknowledges the relevance of this role and the impact it had on her career as an educator (Brigham Young University, 2002). From the beginning, as an elementary teacher in an Edinburg, Texas, public school in 1966, Saracho utilized her keen observation skills to study the ways that children think and learn. She was attuned to the cognitive learning styles of her students and sought to provide an educational environment that would facilitate their optimal development with inclusive practices and playful learning experiences. Importantly, Saracho developed theories about the role of play as an educative tool for teaching (Saracho,1986; Saracho, 1991; Saracho, 1998; Saracho, 2012; Saracho, 2021).

AN INFLUENTIAL SCHOLAR

Olivia Saracho is a prolific writer whose work has contributed significantly to the study of early education and play. Throughout her career in education, as an elementary teacher, lecturer, and professor of education at the University of Maryland, Olivia Saracho influenced the profession with numerous journal articles, books, and conference presentations. She also enjoyed a successful collaboration with her mentor and frequent co-author, Bernard Spodek. Together, they studied learning and play in a variety of educational settings and produced numerous joint publications on cognitive styles, multicultural education, social development, early literacy, and play in education (Saracho & Spodek, 1983; Saracho & Spodek, 1998; Saracho & Spodek, 2002; Saracho & Spodek, 2003a; Saracho & Spodek, 2003b; Saracho & Spodek, 2005; Saracho & Spodek, 2006; Saracho & Spodek, 2007b; Saracho & Spodek, 2008; Saracho & Spodek, 2010; Saracho & Spodek, 1986; Spodek & Saracho, 1987; Spodek & Saracho, 1999).

Cognitive Styles

As a young researcher, Olivia Saracho explored the relationship between educational practice and students' cognitive styles. The concept of cognitive style is a psychological construct that represents learner differences and similarities in how they perceive, learn, contemplate, and critique knowledge. Saracho explains that the two categories within this construct, which has also been described as a psychological differentiation, are known as field dependent and field independent (Saracho & Spodek, 1986; Saracho, 1990; Saracho, 1997).

In addition to studying the relationship between cognitive styles and learning, Saracho conducted research on the relationship between teachers' cognitive styles and students' academic achievement gains (Saracho & Dayton, 1980). Saracho described how teachers benefit when they understand themselves as learners and then apply this self-knowledge to teaching. Specifically, she and her colleagues studied the contrast between field dependent learners and field independent learners. They assessed cognitive characteristics as well as perceptual skills in the categories of intellectual abilities, information processing skills, and subject matter knowledge. Further, they considered personality when looking at variables such as cultural determinants, environment, and responses to instruction (Saracho & Spodek, 1986; Saracho, 1997).

In their studies of elementary students, the authors found that field dependent learners had stronger social skills and responded better to discovery strategies that involved interpersonal relationships, whereas field independent students were less responsive to social cues and tended to prefer lessons that employed a didactic approach. Thus, a field dependent learner would benefit from a lesson that included dramatic play elements but a field independent learner would have a more favorable outcome in a lesson that required fewer social skills (Saracho & Dayton, 1980; Saracho & Spodek, 1986; Saracho, 1997).

Saracho suggests that the quality of education could be improved if teachers facilitated the development of cognitive flexibility and matched cognitive styles with activities and learning tasks (Saracho, 1990; Saracho, 1997). She believes that learners' cognitive styles reveal how they respond to people and solve problems. Although it pertains to the learners' intellectual capacity, it also involves the affective domain since it includes the personality of the child. From her findings, Saracho deduced that a discovery approach to teaching fosters interpersonal relationships between the students and teacher. Further, she emphasized the positive impact of playful, active learning within a social context for all cognitive styles (Saracho, 1990).

Play-based Programs

Traditionally, early learning environments have valued play, yet the implementation of play-based programs differs according to the cultural setting. Saracho (2013) helps teachers understand how play has been interpreted throughout history and that play must be considered a vital element of education. Although the interpretation of playful learning can vary, it is important for practioners to grasp the nature of play and learn how to fully utilize it in a classroom setting (Saracho & Spodek, 1998). Furthermore, Saracho states that play fuels the creative process since the dynamic elements of mystery and humor are consistently found in imaginative play (Saracho, 1986; Saracho & Spodek, 1984).

Olivia Saracho (2012, 2021) emphasized the importance of play and playful learning in both editions of her textbook, *An Integrated Play-Based Curriculum for Young Children.* In the text, which represent a culmination of years of academic research and pedagogical experience, Olivia Saracho communicates the importance of play to practitioners and shares information about the history, principles, and implementation of play-based curriculums. (Saracho, 2012; Saracho, 2021).

Further, Saracho provides guidance for meeting the needs of children by matching their interests with corresponding activities in literacy, math, science, music, art, and spatial perception. She offers suggestions for methods to scaffold play behaviors in a variety of content areas. With a focus on inquiry, Olivia Saracho inspires teachers of young children to provide meaningful experiences with a playful approach (Saracho, 2012, Saracho, 2021).

Multicultural Perspectives

Recent findings suggest that young children's playful experiences are critical to their cognitive processes, so effective early childhood practices can boost the academic potential of children in poverty. Since many children are from linguistically and culturally diverse families, teachers must implement inclusive practices. For example, when a child brings toys from their own culture into the classroom for a culture box, the items will become familiar to the other students and thus assimilate into the natural context of the social setting. Teachers must strive to include elements of each child's culture in the learning community with activities like field trips, guest speakers, art projects, and culture boxes that represent authentic aspects of culture represented in their classroom (Saracho & Spodek,1983; Saracho & Gerstl,1992; Saracho, 2021).

When Saracho studied second language learners who were in the process of adapting to a new culture, she found that they go through four stages: bewilderment, rejection, assimilation, and acculturation. Bewilderment refers to their initial shock as they enter an environment that functions in an unfamiliar language. Secondly, they experience a feeling of rejection since the new setting is such a contrast to their previous environment, as if they are rejected for coming from a different place. Next, they enter the third stage of assimilation in which they adopt components of the new culture into their lives. Finally, children become acculturated. With acculturation, they are able to function in two languages, adopt the play behaviors and dress of the new culture, and comfortably transition from one cultural setting to another (Brigham Young University, 2002).

Facilitating Literacy through Play

In response to the growing demand by policy makers and educational administrators to provide literacy instruction to children at increasingly younger ages, preschool and kindergarten teachers are required to teach students to read. To meet the needs of teachers of young children, Olivia Saracho provides play-based literacy learning activities in both editions of *An Integrated Play-Based Curriculum for Young Children.* In the directives for the activities, which are designed to foster a love of literature and promote emergent reading skills, Saracho includes playful components with movement, imaginative verse, and drama that motivate children to engage with stories through play (Saracho, 2012, Saracho, 2021).

The study of early literacy involves cultural components and the expectations for very young children in various demographics have evolved over time. Now, in the twenty-first century, children are expected to learn how to read either before or during their kindergarten year, at age five. To define the concept of literacy, The National Council of Teachers of English states,

> Because technology has increased the intensity and complexity of literate environments, the 21st century demands that a literate person possess a wide range of abilities and competencies, many literacies. (NCTE, 2013)

Thus, parents and teachers of young children must match their efforts to prepare children for reading with current expectations for literate students, while also balancing their need for time to play (Copple & Bredekamp, 2009; Saracho, 2021).

Saracho highlights the impact of the family on children's acquisition of literacy. She cites literacy studies that validate the significance of parental involvement in the development of emergent reading skills when they participate in oral language activities, read aloud to children, and model reading habits. She states that the federal government should play a role in promoting education at home by supporting parent education programs, family literacy programs, policies that promote family literacy, and family literacy interventions (Saracho, 2017). Furthermore, the systems that support emergent literacy develop through social activities and play experiences. When children play, they become meaning makers as they use language in literate ways to explore vocabulary and negotiate with peers (Saracho & Spodek, 2006; Saracho, 2008).

In the connectionist view of development, children's readiness for literacy learning can be enhanced by preparatory activities that are implemented by influential adults or more advanced peers. From this mainstream perspective, games and toys that promote phonemic awareness are linked to the ability to apply these skills to the recognition of words and, ultimately, the ability to read. Activities that support this form of early literacy training include alphabet books and puzzles, letter bingo, matching games, and flash cards (Crawford, 1995).

Saracho, however, emphasizes a holistic approach to promoting literacy that involves an immersive and dynamic process with multimodal methods, which begins in the home long before formal schooling. She advocates for children to develop extensive language and literacy skills in the home with literacy interactions that include strong verbal communication practices, reading strategies, a print-rich environment, play materials, read-aloud sessions, and story extensions in the form of sociodramatic play experiences (Saracho, 2002; Saracho & Spodek, 2008).

Additionally, Saracho provided suggestions for teachers of young children to extend the development of language and literacy in formal early learning environments. She communicates the importance of promoting both receptive (listening, reading) and expressive (speaking, writing) literacy behaviors (Saracho, 2004). Saracho notes that young children display literacy-like behaviors when they pretend to read, scribble unconventional messages, respond to storytime activities, and recognize environmental print, and that these actions occur long before they reach the classroom (Saracho, 2003; Saracho & Spodek, 2010).

Teachers can support literacy play by providing experiences such as read-aloud sessions that include verbal interactions, games and activities that focus on sound patterns, opportunities to engage in puppet shows, participation in reader's theater, interactive board games, and literature-based art projects such as collages, dioramas, and sculpture. Individual differences must be considered as well as developmental abilities (Saracho, 2021).

As children begin to recognize the purpose of reading, they are motivated to explore the understanding of content, pursue skills related to decoding the text, and learn the relationships between print and speech. Additionally, Saracho explains, "These literacy experiences assist them to see the connection between (a) print and objects, (b) print and speech, and (c) letters and their sounds" (Saracho, 2021, p. 197).

Teacher Preparation

Olivia Saracho proclaims that in order to effectively implement play-based curriculums, teacher preparation programs need to provide appropriate trainings. Preservice teachers must be able to comprehend both the importance of play as an educative force and how to implement methods that will effectively scaffold students' thinking process during play (Evans & Saracho,

1992). Saracho (2003) describes how children demonstrate their thinking as they organize their physical space and participate in play behaviors (p.75), and implores teachers to harness the power of play in teaching and learning.

Obviously, play has been included in formal early learning environments since their inception. However, research studies reveal discrepancies in practice. For example, teachers may offer perfunctory verbal support for play but may not provide sufficient opportunities for students to engage in self-selected activities. Perhaps they set up props in the play environment and even take notes on the play activities. However, children need specific guidance in the form of explicit interventions implemented by a skilled educator (Saracho, 1991; Saracho, 2003; Saracho, 2013).

Whether their actions reflect a lack of knowledge or adequate training, the result is that children in the care of unprepared teachers will not receive the appropriate support to reach their optimal potential. To alleviate this dilemma, Olivia Saracho petitioned recognized scholars to educate teachers of young children about the benefits of play in the context of best practice by contributing to *Contemporary Perspectives on Play in Early Childhood.* Readers of this volume can utilize the contents as a resource to help them enhance their teaching practice and implement activities for educational play (Saracho, 2003).

CONCLUSION

Throughout her work, Olivia Saracho communicates the value of play as a way for learners to express their thoughts, represent ideas, and experiment with new concepts. She portrays play as the basis for inquiry in all of the academic content areas and shares examples that illuminate the connections between active play and knowledge acquisition.

Additionally, Saracho emphasizes her viewpoint that teachers need appropriate training in order to facilitate the process of learning through play and to maximize the benefits of a play-based curriculum. The contributions that Olivia Natividad Saracho has made to the study of play will continue to influence educators, parents, and future scholars of play for many years to come.

REFERENCES

Brigham Young University (2002). McKay School of Education Speaker Series: Olivia N. Saracho. https://education.byu.edu/tell/transcriptions/may_2002/olivia_saracho.html.

Copple, C., & Bredekamp, S. (2009). *Developmentally appropriate practice in early childhood programs serving children from birth to age 8.* National Association for the Education of Young Children.

Crawford, P. (1995). Early literacy: Emerging perspectives. *Journal of Research in Childhood Education. 10*(1), 71-86. Doi: 10.1080/02568549509594689.

Evans, R., & Saracho, O.N. (1992). *Teacher preparation for early childhood education.* Gordon & Breach Science Publishers.

National Council of Teachers of English. (2013). *The NCTE definition of 21*st *century literacies.* http://www2.ncte.org/statement/21stcentdefinition/.

Saracho, O.N. (1984). Play and young children's learning. In B. Spodek (Ed.), *Today's kindergarten: Exploring the knowledge base, expanding the curriculum.* (pp. 91-109). New York: Teachers College Press.

Saracho, O.N. (1990). *Cognitive style and early education.* New York: Gordon & Breach Science Publishers.

Saracho, O.N. (1991). The role of play in the early childhood curriculum. In B. Spodek & O. N. Saracho (Eds.). *Yearbook of early childhood education: Issues in early childhood curriculum*, Vol. II (pp. 86-105). Teachers College Press.

Saracho, O. N. (1997). *Teachers and students' cognitive styles in early childhood education.* Greenwood Publishing Group, Inc.

Saracho, O. N. (1998). *Multiple perspectives on play in early childhood education.* State University of New York Press.

Saracho, O. N. (2002). *Contemporary perspectives in literacy in early childhood education*, Volume 2. Information Age Publishing.

Saracho, O. N. (2003). Young children's play and cognitive style. In O. N. Saracho and B. Spodek (Eds.), *Contemporary perspectives on play in early childhood* (pp. 75-96). Information Age.

Saracho, O. N. (2004). Supporting literacy-related play: Roles for teachers of young children. *Early Childhood Education Journal*, 31, 201-206.

Saracho, O. N. (2008). Growing up literate with families. In S. Kitano (Ed.) *Promoting child rearing support system: Connecting families, institutions, and communities* (p. 32). Minerva Publishing Co. LTD.

Saracho, O. N. (2012). *An integrated play-based curriculum for young children.* Taylor & Francis.

Saracho, O. N. (2013). The preparation of early childhood teachers: Fundamental components of a teacher education program. In R. Reutzel (Ed.), *The handbook of research-based practice in early childhood education* (pp. 27-45). Guilford Press.

Saracho, O. N. (2017). Literacy in the twenty-first century: Children, families and policy. *Early Child Development and Care, 187*, 3-4, 630-643.

Saracho, O. N. (2021). *An integrated play-based curriculum for young children*, 2nd edition. Taylor & Francis.

Saracho, O. N., & Dayton, C. M. (1980). Relationship of teachers' cognitive styles to pupils' academic achievement gains. *Journal of Educational Psychology, 79,* 4, 544-549.

Saracho, O.N., & Gerstl, C. K. (1992). Learning differences among at-risk minority students. In H. C. Waxman, J. W. Felix, J. E. Anderson, and H. P. Baptiste (Eds.) *Improving the education of at-risk students.* (pp. 105-135). Corwin Press, Inc.

Saracho, O. N., & Spodek, B. (Eds.) (1983). *Understanding the multicultural experience in early childhood education*. National Association for the Education of Young Children.

Saracho, O. N., & Spodek, B. (1986). Cognitive style and children's learning: Individual variation in cognitive processes. In L. G. Katz (Ed.), *Current topics in early childhood education*, Vol. VI, pp. 177-194. Ablex.

Saracho, O. N., & Spodek, B. (1998). *Multiple perspectives on play in early childhood education*. State University of New York Press.

Saracho, O. N., & Spodek, B. (2002). *Contemporary perspectives in literacy in early childhood*, Vol. II. Information Age Publishing.

Saracho, O. N., & Spodek, B. (2003a). *Studying teachers in early childhood settings*, Vol. IV. Information Age Publishing.

Saracho, O. N., & Spodek, B. (2003b). *Contemporary perspectives on play in early childhood*, Vol. III. Information Age Publishing.

Saracho, O.N., & Spodek, B. (2005). *Contemporary perspectives on families, communities and schools for young children*. Vol. VI. Information Age Publishing.

Saracho, S. & Spodek, B. (2006) Young children's literacy-related play, Early Child Development and Care, 176:7, 707-721, DOI: 10.1080/03004430500207021.

Saracho, O. N., & Spodek, B. (2008). Oracy: Social facets of language learning. In R. Evans & D. Jones (Ed.) *Metacognitive approaches to developing oracy*. (pp. 127–137. Routledge.

Saracho, O.N., & Spodek, B. (2010). *Contemporary perspectives in language and cultural diversity in early childhood education*. Information Age Publishing.

Spodek, B., & Saracho, O.N. (1987). The challenge of educational play. In D. Bergen (Ed.), *Play as a learning medium*. (pp. 9-22). Exeter, NH: Heinemann.

Spodek, B., & Saracho, O. N. (1999). *Early childhood education: Issues in early childhood curriculum*. Educator's International Press, Inc.

16

Valora Washington

1953–

Vivien L. Geneser and Jerletha McDonald

Valora Washington.

Play is an important pathway to learning and is essential to child development.

On a trip to West Africa during the early nineteen-seventies, a college student observed the ways that children served their communities—playful yet with a sense of purpose. Intrigued, she sought to learn about the elements that influenced their behaviors. The youthful traveler, Valora Washington, is now a distinguished author, speaker, and international leader in the early childhood profession who advocates for play in early learning environments. When she reflects on that experience, she realizes that it was a pivotal moment in the trajectory of her life's work. In the ensuing decades, she embarked on an illustrious career and garnered dozens of awards, publications, and honorary degrees while also remaining true to her quest to understand and advocate for young children (Washington, 2021).

ARCHITECT OF CHANGE

Valora Washington grew up in a tight-knit community in Ohio, where she experienced the benefits of intergenerational relationships and continuity of care, with relatives who served as volunteers for churches and schools. Valora fondly recalls doing homework at the kitchen table, reading hundreds of library books each summer, playing with friends in the neighborhood, and participating in community activities with her family (Washington, Gadson, & Amel 2015).

Sadly, she also recalls the tragic loss of four young neighbors, siblings who had lived in an apartment above a local bar, and died in a fire. She lamented her inability to rebuild the physical structure in which they perished but felt called to reform the societal infrastructure that contributed to their demise. While watching the funeral procession of their diminutive caskets, she vowed to try to prevent future losses in the community by improving conditions for the poor. Thus, Valora Washington was motivated to become an architect of change (Bernhardt, 2014).

From this nurturing environment, Valora launched an academic career, attending Michigan State University on a scholarship, completing a doctorate at Indiana University by age 24, and achieving the rank of tenured professor at the University of North Carolina at Chapel Hill by age 30. Later, she was granted the position of vice president at Antioch College in Ohio. Soon thereafter, she was recruited by the Kellogg Foundation to serve as a subject matter expert in the field of early childhood education. She also became their first black vice president. Through the years, Valora Washington has contributed to many organizations that serve young children, such as the National

Head Start Program and the Center for Enhancing Early Learning Outcomes (CEELO). Additionally, she served as CEO for the Council for Professional Recognition which facilitates the Child Development Associate Credentialing Program (CDA) and founded the Community Advocates for Young Learners (CAYL) Institute (Bernhardt, 2014).

Play Equity

The topic of equity is central to the work of Valora Washington. During her service as a professor, she studied the effects of racism on young learners and published numerous articles on desegregation and the experiences of black children in American public schools. She conducted research studies that looked at children's racial identity, the role of teacher behaviors, and teachers' perceptions of race (Washington, 1976; Washington, 1979; & Washington, 1982).

Washington approached the racism dilemma with an affinity for solution-oriented practice so, with the intent of helping education professionals diminish racism, she developed training programs, published articles, and gave presentations at conferences that promoted anti-bias curriculum and instruction (Washington, 1979; Washington, 1981; Washington & Bailey 1995).

Washington states,

> More than ever in this era of twin pandemics—coronavirus and heightened sense of racial inequities—play is vital to support young children. To support children's emotional and social growth during these challenging times, families and programs must be intentional about helping children to find joy, and to understand the world, through their play. We must even more intentionally ensure that children's worlds are filled with rich language, active movements, music, laughter, dance, manipulatives, and opportunities to explore and create. We must take care they are not exposed to excessive, developmentally inappropriate daily news about death or racism. While the value of play is strong for all children, it is particularly essential for children of color as they may need tools to cope with the additional stress or fear of microaggressions, adultification bias, or racialized violence. (2020)

It's Magic!

As you enter a high-quality early environment you may notice a feeling of excitement that tells you it is ideal for children. According to Roger and Bonnie Neugebauer, *it's magic*! Written in the foreword of *The New Early Childhood Professional: A Step by Step Guide to Overcoming Goliath*, they are referring to the ambiance of an environment that transcends the tedious text of a basic checklist for quality (Washington, et al, 2015, p. ix).

Similarly, when Washington (2020) speaks of the joy that children bring to the world and how they express joyfulness during play, she highlights the importance of providing spaces where children can play freely. Washington (2021) also emphasizes the importance of preparing teachers of young children to understand the value of play. She cites research to support play-based programs that facilitate the development of social-emotional skills, since they promote readiness for kindergarten (144).

The role of the teacher is key to the success of a play-based program and intentionality is a necessary component for refining the skills of effective teaching. Washington (2021) asserts that teachers who practice with intentionality and hone their observation skills will be better able to engage in powerful interactions with young learners, which leads to the relationships that are so essential to a positive learning environment (45).

Washington laments the fact that

> historically in our country, people who work with children under the age of five haven't had a lot of training because many people assume that anyone can teach young children. People think it is just kind of an extension of mothering. But actually, that's not true. Research shows that working with children in a particular way strengthens opportunities for learning and can have a lifetime impact on them in all kinds of ways. (2020)

Furthermore, Washington states,

> A series of substantial and careful reviews of high-quality programs, including Head Start, report benefits from these programs for children and their families in terms of school readiness, self-esteem, and motivation for achievement. In fact, research shows that children develop early literacy skills more readily when parents read to them regularly and when teachers are educated about how children acquire language and literacy skills. And when their teachers are educated about how children acquire language and literacy skills, they use that knowledge in the classroom. (2020)

The benefits of an excellent early childhood program cannot be overstated. Valora Washington reminds us that

> when children receive a high-quality early education, they earn more money as adults, are more likely to be homeowners, less likely to drop out of school, and less likely to become teen parents. The impact of a good early childhood education benefits society as a whole. (2020)

Play and Development

In all of her work, Washington communicates the importance of understanding the relationship between play and development. She stresses that

> new research and technologies have illuminated our understanding of brain development and how children learn. Yet with all the information available to us, we—as a country—seem to *know* more than we *do*. Our knowledge about how the brain grows and develops has grown exponentially in the past five years. This is due in part to technologies such as positron-emission tomography (PET) scans. Unlike the skeletal system, the child's brain wiring is not fully determined before birth. It develops in direct response to environmental input. Brain growth occurs most quickly and easily in the first three years of life, and affects speech, movement, and social relationships. While it may be more difficult to make neural connections after the age of nine, the brain continues to have the potential to grow and change. But the truth is that research consistently and increasingly demonstrates the benefits of play. The link between play and academic and social success has been firmly established. Play is an important pathway to learning, essential to child development. (2020)

Washington (2021) encourages parents and teachers to play with children and to scaffold their ideas during play sessions in order to encourage them to investigate, explore, and discuss their experiences. Adults can help children extend their inquiry by providing new materials, validating their discoveries, and scaffolding the conversations, all of which contribute to the growth of attentional skills (145). Moreover, she states,

> the pathways for emotional development—how the child feels and behaves—grow in the limbic area of the brain. When adults play with children, they should model the attributes of curiosity and wonder, for the purpose of facilitating problem-solving skills. (Washington, 2020)

Overcoming Goliath

Valora Washington strives to provide tools for early childhood professionals to become agents of change for the profession. In their 2015 publication, Valora Washington, Brenda Gadson, and Kathryn Amel compared the struggles of early educators to the biblical plight of David and Goliath and compiled a volume of guidelines for early educators (David) to stave off the challenges wrought by public opinions (Goliath). They acknowledge the overwhelming nature of the task of transforming community perceptions and provide directives to empower early childhood professionals to become architects of change (Washington, et al, 2015, p. 17).

An important recommendation is for teachers to learn how to describe play as an essential component of healthy development. The authors assert that practitioners need to be ready for parents who favor an emphasis on strict academics. An articulate teacher will be proficient in the benefits of play for the sake of supporting play-based programs, thus able to share examples of the ways that children learn through play (Washington, et al, 2015, p. 108).

Washington (2021) states that she has always designed early education programs that are child-driven, with an emphasis on play, curiosity, and constructivist learning (36). While serving as the CEO for the Council for Professional Recognition, Valora Washington successfully implemented a transformation of the Child Development Associate (CDA) Credential™ program, which helps thousands of early childhood educators attain their CDA credential each year. By expanding the availability of the program, they sought to professionalize the early educator workforce and educate CDA candidates about the value of play. Valora Washington collaborated with other leaders in the early childhood field to improve the credentialing program and, as a result, the CDA has greatly increased in enrollment, certificate attainment, and renewals in the United States and in many other countries (Bernhardt, 2014).

In another show of commitment to the early education profession, Valora Washington cofounded an organization, Community Advocates for Young Learners (CAYL) Institute in 2004. The CAYL Institute aspires to provide a forum for educators to connect with the community and advocate for the profession. Washington states, "we equip leaders in early care and education to be architects of change for all children" (Washington, et al, 2015). She also uses CAYL as a platform to communicate the importance of play and co-created the tradition of weekly playgroups as an effective way to foster a sense of belonging in the program. By participating in these family-friendly events, students, staff, and parents expand relationships, thereby strengthening connections (Washington et al., 2015, p.79).

Twenty-First Century Play

Many parents, educators, community stakeholders, and medical professionals are concerned about the state of play in the twenty-first century. The lack of recognition for the value of play in American culture is evidenced by the decline in free play in early education settings, an increase in screen time among young children, and the decrease in time for recess in public schools (Jarrett, 2013; Washington, 2021; Yogman, Garner, & Hutchinson, 2018). Valora Washington (2021) also voices apprehension about the decrease in outdoor play. Citing statistics from the National Recreation and Park Association, she reports that children spend seven minutes or less in unstructured outdoor play but seven hours or more with technological devices daily (44).

Additionally, Washington and colleagues (2015) express concern over the dilemma of efficacy, such as children who prioritize screen time because they don't know how to play (p. 12). She believes that in the push for an emphasis on academics in preschool, programs have diminished the concept of play in ways that "defeat the potential rigor and intentionality of high-quality, developmentally appropriate practice" (Washington et al., 2015, p. 37). Early education settings that implement instructional methods in alignment with the research-based principles set forth by the National Association for the Education of Young Children allow time for play in their programs (Copple & Bredekamp, 2009).

Looking Ahead

Valora Washington integrated the topic of play into all of her publications, programs, and curriculum throughout her career. She reflects,

> Because play is so enjoyable, many family members and some educators think that fun equals frivolous. In this view, play is a distraction from learning. Even those who concede that play can be useful may be quick to cut play from programming in favor of more academic pursuits. Unfortunately, "From an educational policy perspective, free play may have a hard time surviving in an era where testing and accountability are the forefront of the educational agenda." (2020)

Now semi-retired, Valora Washington continues to write, speak at national conferences, and mentor other leaders in the early childhood profession. One of her dynamic proteges, Jerletha McDonald, is the President of the National Family Child Care Association. She credits Valora Washington with providing her with wise counsel when she said, "Don't call me for the sugar-coated answer, I'm going to tell you the real" (Fraga & McDonald, 2021; Geneser, 2020).

CONCLUSION

In a personal communication, Valora Washington stated,

> As educators of young children, we play a critical role in supporting parents, programs, and public policies that improve children's quality of life. Traditionally, early childhood educators have prided themselves on their commitment to promote key values: respect for and inclusion of all children, working to correct inequities, and accountability for child outcomes according to continually evolving professional standards. While the value of play is strong for all children, it is particularly essential for children of color as they may need tools

to cope with the additional stress or fear of microaggressions, adultification bias, or racialized violence. Now, as advocates for what is best for children, we must also help others in our society realize that "school reform" begins at birth. We must use our brain research and best practices to ensure that every child is given an equal opportunity to develop his capabilities. The time is now—and it's up to us. (Washington, 2020)

REFERENCES

Bernhardt, G. (2014). *Profiles in success: Inspiration from executive leaders in the Washington, DC Area, Volume VIII.* Bernhardt Wealth.

Copple, C., & Bredekamp, S. (2009). *Developmentally appropriate practice in early childhood programs serving children from birth to age 8.* National Association for the Education of Young Children.

Fraga, L., & McDonald, J. (2021). Guest Speaker: A Seat at the Table, Episode 3. Child Care Aware of America. https://www.youtube.com/watch?v=uweGEy_d1tM&t=1119s

Geneser, V. (2020). Jerletha McDonald: What is my why? *Early Years, 40,* 3, 10–15.

Jarrett, O. (2013). A Research-Based Case for Recess. US Play Coalition. Clemson.edu.

Washington, V. (1976). "Learning racial identity". In *De-mythologizing the inner-city child*, Edited by Granger, R.C., and Young, J.C., 85–98. National Association for the Education of Young Children.

Washington, V. (1979). The role of teacher behavior in school desegregation. *Educational Horizons*, *57*, 145–51.

Washington, V. (1981). Impact of antiracism/multicultural education training on elementary teachers' attitudes and classroom behavior. *The Elementary School Journal*, n. p.

Washington, V. (1982). Racial differences in teacher perceptions of first and fourth grade pupils on selected characteristics. *The Journal of Negro Education, 51,* 1, 60–72. https://doi.org/10.2307/2294650.

Washington, V. (2020). Personal communication.

Washington, V. (2021). *Changing the game for Generation Alpha: Teaching and raising young children in the 21st century.* Redleaf Press.

Washington, V., Gadson, B., & Amel, K. (2015). *The new early childhood professional: A step by step guide to overcoming Goliath.* Teachers College Press.

Washington, V., & Oyemade Bailey, U. (1995). *Project head start: Models and strategies for the twenty-first century.* Routledge.

Yogman, M., Garner, A., Hutchinson, J., et al. (2018). The power of play: A pediatric role in enhancing development in young children. *Pediatrics, 1,* 142, 3.

17

The United Nations Convention on the Rights of the Child and Article 31

Reece Wilson

Play, according to Scales, Almay, Nicolopoulou, and Ervin-Tripp (1991), is, "that absorbing activity in which healthy young children participate with enthusiasm and abandon" (p. 15). Fromberg (1992) describes play as being both pleasurable and intrinsically motivated. The United Nations Convention on the Rights of the Child (UNCRC) (1989), in General Comment 17 (2013) (general comments provide analysis and interpretations of certain articles contained in the UNCRC), defines play as

> any behavior, activity or process initiated, controlled and structured by children themselves; it takes place whenever and wherever opportunities arise . . . play itself is non-compulsory, driven by intrinsic motivation and undertaken for its own sake, rather than as a means to an end. Play involves the exercise of autonomy, physical, mental or emotional activity, and has the potential to take infinite forms either in groups or alone. These forms will change and be adapted throughout the course of childhood.
>
> The key characteristics of play are fun, uncertainty, challenge, flexibility, and non-productivity. Together, these factors contribute to the enjoyment it produces and the consequent incentive to continue to play. While play is often considered non-essential, the Committee reaffirms that it is a fundamental and vital dimension of the pleasure of childhood, as well as an essential component of physical, social, cognitive, emotional and spiritual development.

This definition of play, contained in General Comment 17, is central to Article 31 of the UNCRC. The focus of this chapter is a description of Article 31, how the ideas and concepts that make up this article are currently viewed by nations, and how the play community can advocate for the ideals that comprise Article 31.

THE UNITED NATION'S CONVENTION ON THE RIGHTS OF THE CHILD

The United Nation's Convention on the Rights of the Child (UNCRC), adopted by the United Nations General Assembly on November 20, 1989, is a human rights treaty that supports the rights of children worldwide. The UNCRC has been ratified by 193 countries, leaving the United States of America the only country in the world that has not ratified the Convention. The UNCRC supports the idea that children have the right to participate in decisions regarding their future as well as the right to express their opinions. The UNCRC is comprised of 54 articles that recognize the rights of all children to develop physically, mentally, and socially.

A sampling of these 54 articles include articles that address societal issues such as child trafficking, drug abuse, child labor, sexual exploitation, health and health services, and the right to an education. Other articles address basic rights of the child including the child's right to non-discrimination, freedom of expression, freedom of thought, privacy, and freedom of association.

Article 31

While these articles address issues of great importance to all children, Article 31, the focus of this chapter, focuses on play and the right to play for all children. Article 31 (1989) states

> that every child has the right to rest and leisure, to engage in play and recreational activities appropriate to the age of the child and to participate freely in cultural life and the arts.
>
> That member governments shall respect and promote the right of the child to participate fully in cultural and artistic life and shall encourage the provision of appropriate and equal opportunities for cultural, artistic, recreational and leisure activity.

Unfortunately, Article 31 has become known as "the forgotten article of the Convention." Very few of the national reports to the UN Committee (required by signatories of the Convention) have included article 31 in their reports and those which have done so have largely focused on children's physical activity and not embraced all components of the article. In order to provide guidance to governments in implementing Article 31, the UN, in early 2013, developed and adopted General Comment 17.

The International Play Association: Promoting the Child's Right to Play has produced a summary of General Comment 17 (2013) which details the key pieces of this general comment. The summary begins by listing the three "key components" of Article 31 which include 1. Play and Recreation, 2. Involvement in Cultural and Artistic Life, and 3. Rest and Leisure. IPA tells us these parts are interdependent. They "are all linked and together serve to describe conditions necessary to protect the unique and evolving nature of childhood" (p. 2).

Summary

The summary then explains the conditions needed if the rights described in Article 31 are to be fully met. These include 1. A safe environment, free from violence and social harm, as well as traffic and pollution, 2. Freedom from social exclusion, discrimination, stress, and prejudice, 3. Time for rest and leisure, including time not directed by adults, and 4. Space to explore outdoors, with the support of adults, when needed.

What challenges will face nations as they address Article 31? The IPA summary tells us the following issues are front and center as governments work to bring this work to fruition. These issues include the lack of recognition of the importance of play, pressure for educational achievement, the proliferation of technology, unsafe environments, and the resistance to let children use public spaces. As nations work to address Article 31, there is one lone nation that has not ratified the UNCRC treaty.

The United States of America and the UNCRC

The United States of America is the only nation that has not ratified the UNCRC. America signed the treaty in 1995, but never ratified it. Once a country ratifies a treaty, it is legally bound to follow the document.

Why hasn't the UNCRC been ratified by the United States? According to Rothschild (2017), "Some Republican senators in the U.S. have strongly resisted ratification, stating that the treaty undermines U.S. sovereignty in matters of law, and parental sovereignty at home." Opponents to the UNCRC believe that by ratifying the treaty, laws in the United States may be challenged. These include laws governing corporal punishment by parents, incarceration of juveniles, rights of same-sex parents, and access to contraception by minors.

Clearly, there are many hurdles to be traversed as governments work to meet the tenets of Article 31, and, in the case of the United States of America, to ratify the treaty. The International Play Association summary gives us a guiding document to make this important work a reality.

Advocacy

What can we do to promote Article 31? The information that follows was developed by the International Play Association (Admin, 2012) and offers suggestions to advocate for Article 31.

- ***It is important for Article 31 to be included in the national UNCRC implementation plans that are mandatory when a nation ratifies the UN Convention.***

  IPA Branches, member groups and all relevant groups should promote the inclusion of Article 31 in national plans or through their official report or through their NGO (non-governmental organization) coalition.

  Locate your national NGO coalition, or coalitions, which produces a regular report to the UN Committee at about the same time as their national government one (approximately every five years).While the UN Committee encourages such coalitions, not all countries yet have them. Reports from single or groups of NGOs are therefore also received.

  IPA representation on NGO coalitions, or at least a close contact with them, would be an advantage for greater recognition and implementation of Article 31.
- ***The range of government ministries or departments, which should be included in Article 31 implementation, is a particular challenge. It makes sense for Article 31 supporters to help identify key players and organize discussion groups about its implementation priorities.***

  Given the Article 31 components of rest and leisure, play and recreation, culture and the arts, there would be a wide range of government departments involved. Those with a responsibility in this field would include, for example, education, recreation, health, social services, labor, social and physical planning, culture, and sports, as well as those concerned with transport, housing and sanitation.
- ***A goal of IPA Branches and groups would be to support the development of a national policy or framework for Article 31.***

  Identify the nation's relevant government departments—as above—and other key national non-government organizations, such as IPA, and encourage comprehensive discussions about Article 31.

  Implementation of the Convention through policy is essential. It can be developed to interpret or build on legislation, or to set out the direction of government or non-governmental organizations in the absence of legislation.

  Since policy also guides the delivery of programs and services, implementation of the Convention becomes possible through day-to-day practice. (For example: Wales Play Policy, 2002.)

- ***Orientation and training on Article 31 should be accessible for all professionals working with or for children.***

  Is the status of national training, particularly with regard to play, known to IPA Branches, member groups and all relevant groups involved in Article 31?

  What steps could be taken to improve this? Do you have information that would be useful to other countries?

CONCLUSION

As these advocacy strategies by IPA convey, it is imperative that all people who care about the welfare of the world's children work together at the local, state, national, and international level. For example, local and state affiliates of NAEYC could network with groups such as IPAUSA to contact to lawmakers to influence others in the government to work toward ratification of the UNCRC, including Article 31, by the United States of America.

REFERENCES

Admin, I. S. (2012, May 01). UN Convention on the Rights of the Child. Retrieved January 09, 2018, from http://ipaworld.org/childs-right-to-play/uncrc-article-31/un-convention-on-the-rights-of-the-child-1/

Convention on the Rights of the Child General comment No. 17 [PDF]. (2013, May 29). United Nations Committee on the Rights of the Child. General Comment (#17) Home » Child's Right to Play » Article 31 » General Comment (#17). (2013, April 17). Retrieved January 09, 2018, from http://ipaworld.org/childs-right-to-play/article-31/general-comment-17/

Fromberg, D. P. (1992). A review of research on play. In C. Seefeldt (Ed.), *The early childhood curriculum: A review of current research* (2nd ed., pp. 42–84). Teachers College Press.

Rothschild, A. (2017, May 2). Is America Holding Out on Protecting Children's Rights? *The Atlantic*.

Scales, B., Almay, M. C., Nicolopoulou, A., & Ervin-Tripp, S. (1991). *Play and the social context of development in early care and education* (pp. 15–31). Teachers College, Columbia Univ.

About the Editor and Contributors

David J. Akpata is an Early Childhood Specialist and a reviewer for the *Early Years* journal. He gives presentations at Early Childhood conferences and is the author of several articles pertaining to fatherhood. His research interests also include Critical Race Theory in American education.

Jerry Aldridge is professor emeritus of early childhood education at the University of Alabama at Birmingham. He is the author of numerous books, including *Stealing from the Mother: The Marginalization of Women in Education and Psychology from 1900-2010* (2013) with Lois M. Christensen, and *A Turning Point in Teacher Education: A Time for Resistance, Reflection, and Change* (2019) with James D. Kirylo, both published by Rowman & Littlefield.

LaDonna Atkins, EdD, is a professor in the Department of Human Environmental Sciences at the University of Central Oklahoma. She is a member and past president of the United States Affiliate of the International Play Association (www.ipausa.org) and is also a member of The Association for the Study of Play (TASP). Dr. Atkins is the recipient of the Vanderford Teaching Award and the Neely Excellence in Teaching Award and serves on the research committee for the newly established Oklahoma Clearinghouse for Early Childhood Success.

Joanna Cemore Brigden, PhD, has taught in private and public schools from pre-K through college. She is passionate about defending the child's right to play and serves as a board member for both the Association for the Study of Play and the International Play Association-United States Affiliate. She conducts research in play, creativity, emotional intelligence, service-learning, and teacher perceptions.

Walter F. Drew is a former president of The Association for the Study of Play and is currently researching the benefits of play and art making on aging. For more than forty years he has studied, practiced, and presented *Self-Active Play* experiences as a healing process and wrote *Self-Active Play: Awakens Creativity, Empowers Self Discovery, Inspires Optimism* (2021) with Marcia L. Nell. Dr. Drew's Blocks were chosen Best Toy of the Year in 1982 by the Parents Choice Foundation.

Edith Esparza, PhD is an Associate Professor of Language Education and program director at the University of Medicine and Health Sciences in St. Kitts in the West Indies. She has been an educator and an advocate for bilingual education and for people of color throughout her career. Dr. Esparza is an immigrant from Mexico who is passionate about the historical foundations of bilingual education and giving voices to under-represented communities.

Vivien L. Geneser, PhD has implemented a playful approach to teaching at all levels from preschool to university, most recently as an Associate Professor of Early Childhood education at Texas A&M University-San Antonio (A&M-SA). Dr. Geneser has received many accolades, including a Teaching and Research Excellence Award from the Texas A&M University System. She has served as a co-editor of both *Early Years,* and the *IPAUSA eJournal*, and is the author of numerous articles and book chapters about play and education.

Marcy Guddemi, PhD, MBA, and national consultant, is widely recognized as an expert in early education, learning though play, and developmental assessment. As former executive director of Gesell Institute of Child Development at Yale, Dr. Guddemi led her team promoting the principles of child development in all decision making for young children. She has held teaching positions at University of South Carolina, University of South Florida, and Texas State University. In the private sector, she held corporate positions at KinderCare (VP), CTB/McGraw-Hill, Harcourt, and Pearson. Guddemi is an active member and officer of the American Affiliate of the International Play Association (IPAUSA) and Advisory Board Member for Let's Play America.

Shelley Harris, PhD, is an Associate Professor and Graduate Program Coordinator in Curriculum and Instruction at Texas A&M University-Central Texas. Her research agenda includes topics pertaining to effective teaching modalities, community-based initiatives, literacy, and play. Dr. Harris has numerous publications including *Effective Teaching: Educators Perspective of Meaning Making in Higher Education* (2018), and has presented at state, national and international conferences.

Blythe Hinitz, PhD, is Distinguished Professor Emeritus of Elementary and Early Childhood Education at the College of New Jersey. She is the editor of *Impeding Bullying Among Young Children in International Group Contexts* (2018) and *The Hidden History of Early Childhood Education* (2013), co-author of *History of Early Childhood Education* (2000; 2011), a foundational text in the field, and author of numerous book chapters and journal articles. She is an Exchange Exceptional Master Leader.

Olga S. Jarrett is Professor Emerita, Department of Early Childhood and Elementary Education at Georgia State University. She taught child development, science and social studies methods, and a PhD seminar on play. A past president of The Association for the Study of Play (TASP) and IPAUSA, she was also recipient of play awards from TASP, IPAUSA, US Play Coalition, and Play, Policy, and Practice Interest forum of National Association for the Education of Young Children.

Debra L. Lawrence has over forty years in the field of early care and education. Her commitment to the profession includes service to the Colorado Association for the Education of Young Children as past president, former policy chair for National Association for the Education of Young Children's governing board, and current president of the International Play Association, USA affiliate. Debra is an associate professor in teacher preparation programs at Delaware County Community College, the author of *How Public Investment Contributes to High-Quality Early Childhood Programs: Lessons from Pennsylvania*, contributing author to *Learning from Head Start*, and the co-author of "What We Learned from the Pandemic," published in the July/August 2021 *Exchange Magazine.*

Jerletha McDonald is a social entrepreneur, consultant, trainer, national speaker, president of the National Association of Family Child Care, and member of the Texas Governor Early Learning Council. Jerletha is also the founder and CEO of the Arlington DFW Child Care Professionals and Radio Host of the *Jerletha McDonald Show: Everything Child Care!* In December of 2020, Jerletha McDonald and Dr. Valora Washington participated in a StoryCorps interview for the American Folklife Center, which is available in the archives at www.StoryCorps.org.

Mary Ruth Moore, PhD, is Professor Emerita of Education of the University of the Incarnate Word of San Antonio where she served for twenty-three years. Dr. Moore holds a doctorate in Curriculum and Instruction from the University of Texas. Prior to her work at U.I.W., she taught for twenty-five years in elementary schools. She co-edited *Play in American Life,* Volumes One and Two in honor of Dr. Joe L. Frost with Connie Sabo-Risley.

Matilde A. Sarmiento, EdD, is a teacher at Oyster Adams Bilingual School in Washington, D.C. She strongly believes in the positive impact bilingualism can have on a child's life and their academic performance all while giving them a broader perspective of the world. She is driven by her professional commitment to make sure that when a child walks into her classroom they feel welcomed, loved, and are taught with high expectations to provide them the education they are entitled to.

Jeroen Staring, PhD, retired in 2018 as a teacher of mathematics at secondary schools in the Netherlands. Jeroen holds a Dutch "Candidate" degree in Medicine, a BA in Mathematics Education, two professional Masters (Special Educational Needs, Pedagogy), and an MSc in Social and Cultural Anthropology. His first (2005) dissertation describes the life, work, and technique of F. Matthias Alexander. His second dissertation (2013) describes the early history of the New York City Bureau of Educational Experiments.

John A. Sutterby, PhD, is an Associate Professor at the University of Texas San Antonio. His program area is in early childhood education where he teaches courses on children's play, action research in early childhood, and child development. His research interests include children's play environments, toys, bilingual education, and children's literature.

Josh Thompson, PhD, is a Professor of Early Childhood Education at Texas A&M University-Commerce and a former co-editor of *Early Years*. As a certified Montessori teacher (AMS E1), he serves as a trainer for Dallas Montessori Teacher Education Program, and writes about Montessori and play. He and his wife are active play partners with their twelve grandchildren.

Karen Walker, EdD, is an Assistant Professor of Child and Family Studies at Northwestern State University in Natchitoches, Louisiana. Her research focuses on early literacy and play. She has presented at early childhood education conferences locally, regionally, and internationally—including the United Kingdom, Kenya, and Ireland.

Reece Wilson, PhD, is a faculty member at James Madison University in the Department of Early, Elementary, and Literacy Education. He has served as the director of the Young Children's Program, JMU's early childhood laboratory school. He serves as treasurer for the American Society for the Child's Right to Play and is the co-leader of JMU's study abroad practicum experience in Northern Ireland/Ireland. His research interests include developmentally appropriate practice, early literacy, technology in the early childhood classroom, and play.

Debora Wisneski is the John T. Langan Community Chair of Early Childhood Education at University of Nebraska-Omaha and current president of The Association for the Study of Play. She is co-editor of the text, *Reconsidering the Role of Play in Early Childhood: Toward Social Justice and Equity* (2018). She enjoys community collaborations that create playful spaces for everyone and values time playing with her family and friends.

Kenya Wolff, PhD, is an Assistant Professor in Early Childhood Education and the co-director for the Graduate Center for the Study of Early Learning at the University of Mississippi. Her research focuses on a holistic approach, including work on the benefits of yoga, mindfulness, and anti-bias curriculum. She is also the co-founder of Growing Healthy Minds, Bodies and Communities, which provides curriculum and resources to schools on mindfulness, yoga, gardening, anti-bias, and social-emotional development for young children.

ABOUT THE ARTISTS

Allison Geneser graduated from the University of Texas with a degree in Studio Art. She specializes in portraits and her work has been featured in numerous shows. Additionally, she taught K-12 Art classes in a rural public school. Allison co-owns Lone Star Workshop, an art gallery and gift shop in Lockhart, Texas.

Benjamin Geneser is a carpenter, welder, mechanic, computer technician, and electronics hobbyist. He enjoys drawing, painting, gardening, graphic design projects, and playing with his wonderful dog, Cameron.